11-16-99 74

THE AS/400 EX

Ready-to-Run
RPG/400
Techniques

Julian Monypenny
Roger Pence

A Division of
DUKE COMMUNICATIONS INTERNATIONAL

221 E. 29th Street • Loveland, CO 80538
(800) 621-1544 • (970) 663-4700 • www.29thStreetPress.com

Library of Congress Cataloging-in-Publication Data

Pence, Roger, 1953-
    The AS/400 expert : ready-to-run RPG/400 techniques / by Roger Pence & Julian
Monypenny.
    p. cm.
    Includes index.
    ISBN 1-58304-046-3 (pbk.)
    1. IBM AS/400 (Computer)--Programming. 2. RPG/400 (Computer program language) I.
Monypenny, Julian, 1955- II. Title.
    QA76.8.I25919 P36 1999
    005.2'45--dc21
                                                98-58129
                                                CIP

Published by 29th Street Press
DUKE COMMUNICATIONS INTERNATIONAL
Loveland, Colorado

ISBN 1-58304-046-3

2001 2000 1999 WL 10 9 8 7 6 5 4 3 2 1

To my grandmother, for the joy she spreads around.
-- J.M.

For my grandparents, who taught me that you can do anything if you try.
-- R.P.

Acknowledgments

We'd like to thank Bryan Meyers for his thorough and very helpful job of tech editing this book (and for the routine or two of his we included); Erik Hymel for the code and testing he contributed; Katie Tipton for her hard work on the reference material; Mel Beckman and Paul Conte for always inspiring us to do better; Roger would also like to thank FG, whose encouragement and support is very much appreciated. Julian would also like to thank Janie for her patience while he "burned the candle" working on this book.

Table of Contents

Chapter 1

Introduction

If you are like many programmers, RPG is your bread-and-butter language. We'd like you to think of this book as your strawberry jam.

USING THIS BOOK

Ask any RPG programmer how many programs (s)he ever started from scratch and the answer will universally be, "None." Everybody "borrows" code: code skeletons, /COPY modules, and even old programs, to launch themselves into a new project. We wrote this book to make it easy for you to borrow code. This book contains RPG snippets, routines, subroutines, /COPY modules, and even a little evangelical advice that you can use to write better, faster, and more reliable RPG. Included among the useful offerings here are string-handling routines, error-handling routines, advice for coding API calls, and numeric editing routines.

We don't spend a lot of time explaining concepts. For example, we include code to harness the power of file I/O feedback areas, but we don't explain those feedback areas. Rather, we assume you are at least conversationally familiar with file feedback areas. For any subject on which you think we moved too fast, check the *RPG User Guide* (SC09-1348) and the *RPG Reference Manual* (SC09-1349) for more details about that subject.

STYLE GUIDELINES

This book doesn't provide complete RPG programs, so you may wonder why we worry at all about style guidelines. The answer is consistency, reliability, and readability. With this book, our goal is to provide you with a set of "plug-in" RPG routines for use in your programs with a minimum amount of trouble and naming conflicts. Here are the style guidelines we have used throughout the book:

- Because of RPG's naming limitations, each routine or /COPY member's field names start with a specified two-character prefix. During testing and development, this two-character prefix ensured that these field names never conflicted with our test code. Beware, though, that if these prefixes (which are clearly indicated for each routine or member) conflict with naming conventions in your shop, you'll need to change them before you use these routines. None of the routines are very long and those changes, if necessary, will be minimal.

- We make extensive use of /COPY routines. Some RPG programmers don't like doing this (for whatever reason), but for us, the value of a proven routine, which can be used over and over again, is worth whatever trade-off in inconvenience the /COPY method provides. However, if you don't like our /COPY method, simply use the include facility from SEU (or your editor of choice) to copy the member directly into your source code.

- Because the layout of this book limited us to a minimal RPG line width, we don't use right-hand margin comments in our RPG code. You will, though, find full-line comments where necessary.

- Each routine or member includes an abstract that shows what other module dependencies it includes; what field values it expects; what field values it returns; any special requirements the routine or member may have (such as assuming that an F-spec somewhere declared a file feed-back I/O data structure name); and what side effects, if any, a routine or member may provide. This abstract also clearly shows the member name (if the code shown is in a member of its own) and the two-character prefix that member's fields use.

- Many of the routines and techniques in this book show example RPG snippets using the appropriate code. These snippets are often abridged samples, not complete programs. We use the colon character (:) in column nine in these snippets to indicate where production RPG code would normally be found.

CD-ROM CONTENTS

To make it even easier for you to borrow code, we've included on the accompanying CD-ROM all the routines, subroutines, and /COPY modules that appear in the figures (e.g., Figure 7.1 — ARYSRT Sort Array Template) throughout the book. You can access each figure directly on the CD-ROM. There is a separate directory for each chapter (e.g., ch07 is Chapter 7's directory). Within a chapter's directory are individual .txt files for each figure (e.g., rtrfig7_1.txt is the file that contains Figure 7.1).

Every effort has been made to ensure that the code provided in the book and on the CD-ROM is correct and accurate. However, all code is provided as is, and it is your responsibility to ensure that procedures and techniques used from this book are appropriate for your installation. No warranty is implied or expressed.

Chapter 2

Effective RPG/400 Error Handling

Use these modules to provide standard, flexible error handling in your RPG programs — and an advanced OS/400 API-like error-reporting mechanism.

In this chapter, we provide the foundation for basic RPG error handling. The modules included in this chapter provide the code needed for basic error reporting and for returning errors from OS/400 APIs and user-written programs. Also included is a module to access the program-status data structure (which provides exception/error-handling information available to your RPG program). Like many of the other modules in this book, these modules are provided as /COPY members.

The first member provided, ERRDS (Figure 2.1), offers the data structure OS/400 APIs use to report errors.

FIGURE 2.1
ERRDS RPG Member

```
... 1 ...+... 2 ...+... 3 ...+... 4 ...+... 5 ...+... 6 ...+... 7 ...+... 8
 *-----------------------------------------------------------------------
 * ERRDS - Error data structure returned by APIs
 *
 * Function:
 *   Defines the error data structure returned by OS/400 APIs (or
 *   any similar program).
 *
 * ERRDS  - err_API_DS:
 *    ERRDSZ - err_data_size
 *    ERRDLN - err_data_len
 *    ERRID  - err_ID
 *    ERR016 - err_filler_16
 *    ERRDTA - err_data
 *-----------------------------------------------------------------------
IERRDS      IDS
I I          256                      B   1   40ERRDSZ
I                                     B   5   80ERRDLN
I                                         9  15 ERRID
I                                        16  16 ERR016
I                                        17 272 ERRDTA
```

The following example shows this module being used with the QUSDLTUS (Delete User Space) OS/400 API. To use this module, use /COPY to include it in your RPG program's I-specs and check the value of the ERRDLN field after

calling the API. If the API returns anything but a zero in ERRDLN, an error
occurred using the API.

```
/COPY ERRDS
   :
   :
C                       MOVEL'MYSPC'   USNAM    P
C                       MOVEL'MYLIB'   USLIB    P
 *
C                       CALL 'QUSDLTUS'
C                       PARM           USQNAM
C                       PARM           ERRDS
 *
C           ERRDLN      IFNE 0
   :                    ...Error processing here
C                       ENDIF
```

The PGMSDS module (Figure 2.2) provides the data structure needed to
make the program status data structure available to your RPG programs.

FIGURE 2.2
PGMSDS Program Status Data Structure

```
... 1 ...+... 2 ...+... 3 ...+... 4 ...+... 5 ...+... 6 ...+... 7 ...+... 8
*-----------------------------------------------------------------------
* PGMSDS - Program status data structure
*
* Function:
*    Defines the Program Status data structure which is updated
*    during the execution of an RPG/400 program.
*
* PGMSDS - pgm_sts_DS:
*    PSPGM  - pgm_sts_pgm
*    PSSTS  - pgm_sts_sts
*    PSSTSP - pgm_sts_prev_sts
*    PSSEQ  - pgm_sts_src_seq
*    PSSR   - pgm_sts_subr
*    PSPRMS - pgm_sts_parm_nbr
*    PSTYP  - pgm_sts_msg_type
*    PSNBR  - pgm_sts_msg_nbr
*    PSMSID - psm_sts_msg_id
*    PSMI   - pgm_sts_mch_inst
*    PSARA  - pgm_sts_work_area
*    PSLIB  - pgm_sts_pgm_lib
*    PSDTA  - pgm_sts_msg_data
*    PSID   - pgm_sts_msg_id
*    PSRS1  - pgm_sts_filler1
*    PSFIL  - pgm_sts_file
*    PSFILS - pgm_sts_file_sts
*    PSJOB  - pgm_sts_job
*    PSUSR  - pgm_sts_user
*    PSJOBN - pgm_sts_job_nbr
*    PSJOBD - pgm_sts_job_date
*    PSPGMD - pgm_sts_pgm_date
*    PSPGMT - pgm_sts_pgm_time
*    PSCMPD - pgm_sts_compile_date
*    PSCMPT - pgm_sts_compile_time
*    PSCMPL - pgm_sts_compile_level
*    PSSRCF - pgm_sts_src_file
*    PSSRCL - pgm_sts_src_lib
```

continued

FIGURE **2.2** *CONTINUED*

```
... 1 ...+... 2 ...+... 3 ...+... 4 ...+... 5 ...+... 6 ...+... 7 ...+... 8
 *    PSSRCM - pgm_sts_src_mbr
 *    PSRS2  - pgm_sts_filler2
 *---------------------------------------------------------------------
IPGMSDS        SDS
I                                         1   10 PSPGM
I                                        11   15 PSSTS
I                                        16   20 PSSTSP
I                                        21   28 PSSEQ
I                                        29   36 PSSR
I                                        37  390PSPRMS
I                                        40   42 PSTYP
I                                        43   46 PSNBR
I                                        40   46 PSMSID
I                                        47   50 PSMI
I                                        51   80 PSARA
I                                        81   90 PSLIB
I                                        91  170 PSDTA
I                                       171  174 PSID
I                                       175  200 PSRS1
I                                       201  208 PSFIL
I                                       209  243 PSFILS
I                                       244  253 PSJOB
I                                       254  263 PSUSR
I                                       264  2690PSJOBN
I                                       270  2750PSJOBD
I                                       276  2810PSPGMD
I                                       282  2870PSPGMT
I                                       288  293 PSCMPD
I                                       294  299 PSCMPT
I                                       300  303 PSCMPL
I                                       304  313 PSSRCF
I                                       314  323 PSSRCL
I                                       324  333 PSSRCM
I                                       334  429 PSRS2
```

This data structure reports exception/error-handling information. The data in this structure includes the RPG program's name, the name of the library in which the program is located, the job name and number, and the number of parameters passed to the program. To use this module, use /COPY to include it in your RPG program's I-specs. Examples of using PGMSDS are shown in the next section of this chapter and in the technique provided in Chapter 3.

ADVANCED ERROR HANDLING

Members ERRDS and PGMSDS are simply definitions of standard data structures and are very straightforward; however, the other two members in this chapter are more complex. These members provide two modules: RERDS (Figure 2.3), which is a duplicate of the ERRDS data structure (Figure 2.1) used to return user error information to the calling program; and RERSET (Figure 2.4), which is an error-handling subroutine that uses modules ERRDS and RERDS.

FIGURE 2.3
RERDS RPG Member

```
... 1 ...+... 2 ...+... 3 ...+... 4 ...+... 5 ...+... 6 ...+... 7 ...+... 8
*-----------------------------------------------------------------------------
* RERDS - Return error data structure for user APIs
*
* Function:
*   Defines a copy of the Error data structure, ERRDS, returned
*   by OS/400 APIs, for error handling in user-written
*   programs or APIs.
*
* RERDS  - rtn_err_API_DS:
*   RERDSZ - rtn_err_data_size
*   RERDLN - rtn_err_data_len
*   RERID  - rtn_err_ID
*   RER016 - rtn_err_filler_16
*   RERDTA - rtn_err_data
*-----------------------------------------------------------------------------
IRERDS          DS
I                                       B   1   40RERDSZ
I                                       B   5   80RERDLN
I                                           9  15 RERID
I                                          16  16 RER016
```

FIGURE 2.4
RERSET RPG Member

```
... 1 ...+... 2 ...+... 3 ...+... 4 ...+... 5 ...+... 6 ...+... 7 ...+... 8
*-----------------------------------------------------------------------------
* RERSET - Set return error data structure
*
* Function:
*   Copies the API error data structure ERRDS to the data
*   structure RERDS for return to the calling program, if
*   RERDS was passed to the subprogram.
*
* Requires copy modules:
*   ERRDS  - Error data structure returned by APIs
*   PGMSDS - Program status data structure
*   RERDS  - Return error data structure for user APIs
*
* Expects:
*   ERRDS  - err_API_DS
*   ERRPRM - err_parm_nbr
*   PSPRMS - pgm_sts_parm_nbr
*   RERDS  - rtn_err_API_DS
*
* Returns:
*   RERDS  - rtn_err_API_DS
*
* Example:
*   Return optional error parameter 5 to the caller.
*
C*                    Z-ADD5         ERRPRM
*                     ...
C*                    EXSR RESET
C*                    RETRN
*
*-----------------------------------------------------------------------------
```

continued

FIGURE 2.4 CONTINUED

```
... 1 ...+... 2 ...+... 3 ...+... 4 ...+... 5 ...+... 6 ...+... 7 ...+... 8
C           RERSET    BEGSR
 *
C                     MOVE ERRPRM    ERRPRM 30
 *
 * Compare optional error parameter to number of parameters
 * passed to this program. If error passed, then return with
 * the length of data defined in the calling program
 *
C           PSPRMS    IFGE ERRPRM
 *
C                     Z-ADDERRDSZ    RERDSZ
C                     MOVELERRID     RERID
C                     MOVELERR016    RER016
C           RERDSZ    SUBSTERRDTA:1  RERDTA
 *
C           ERRDLN    IFLE RERDSZ
C                     Z-ADDERRDLN    RERDLN
C                     ELSE
C                     Z-ADDRERDSZ    RERDLN
C                     ENDIF
 *
C                     ENDIF
 *
C                     ENDSR
```

By using the RERDS and RERSET modules, your own programs can implement a flexible, OS/400 API-like error-reporting mechanism. Like that error handling, the error handling provided by subroutine RERSET is optional. Thus, you can build robust error handling into your RPG programs and use it when necessary, but also disregard it when necessary (as might be the case when you call an RPG routine from CL). Subroutine RERSET provides its optional error-handling capabilities by using the PSPRMS field in the PGMSDS data structure. This structure tells RERSET how many parameters were received when the program was called.

To use RERSET error handling in your programs, use /COPY to include the PGMSDS, ERRDS, and RERDS modules in your RPG program's I-specs and use /COPY to include the RERSET module in the subroutine area of your RPG program's C-specs. The optional ERRDS parameter should always be coded at the end of the parameter list. Immediately after the program's parameter list, use the Z-ADD opcode to set the value of the ERRPRM field (which is declared in the RERSET subroutine) to the number of parameters the program normally expects (remember to change this value if you ever modify the program and change the number of parameters). The ERRPRM field will be used by the RERSET subroutine to determine whether the optional error-handling data structure was passed to the program — thus determining whether error-handling information should be passed back to the caller through this structure.

For example, the following first stub of an RPG program calls the second stub (program TEST), passing the error-handling structure. The calling program is then able to interrogate the value of the ERRDLN field to determine whether an error occurred.

```
/COPY ERRDS
 *
C                         CALL 'TEST'
C                         PARM            PARM1
C                         PARM            PARM2
C                         PARM            ERRDS
 :
C            ERRDLN       IFNE 0
 *                        ...Error processing here
C                         ENDIF


 * Program TEST
/COPY PGMSDS
/COPY ERRDS
/COPY RERDS
 *
C            *ENTRY       PLIST
C                         PARM            PARM1
C                         PARM            PARM2
C                         PARM            RERDS
 * Set ERRPRM which indicates number of parameters
 * the program expects     don't forget to do this!
C                         Z-ADD3          ERRPRM
 :
 :
 * This program ends with a call to RERSET to attempt
 * to return any error information available.
C                         EXSR RERSET
C                         MOVE *ON        *INLR
C                         RETRN
 *
/COPY RERSET
```

Let's also assume that you might occasionally call RPG program TEST from a CL program. When calling TEST from a CL program, you can omit the ERRDS parameter (which contains binary fields that are difficult to use in CL):

```
CALL PGM( 'TEST' ) PARM( Parm1, Parm2 )
```

In this case, the contents of Parm1 or Parm2 would need to be used to determine whether an error occurred in program TEST.

The RERSET subroutine provides solutions to two error-handling problems. First, because the error parameter is optional, it may not have been passed to the program, Second, the length of the error data field, RERDTA, in the caller may be shorter than the declared length in RERDS; if RERSET updates all of RERDTA, the area of memory immediately following RERDTA in the caller will be corrupted.

RERSET solves the first problem by comparing the actual number of parameters passed to the program (contained in the PSPRMS field of the

PGMSDS data structure) to the number of the optional error parameters in field ERRPRM, which is set in a program's mainline before calling RERSET (note in the code on page 5 that this value is set to three, which is the number of parameters this stub expects). Setting ERRPRM in the program is very important: By manually setting ERRPRM to the number of parameters a program expects, and then comparing this value to the number of parameters actually received (from the PSPRMS subfield in the PGMSDS data structure), you can determine whether it is safe to return the error structure. RERSET solves the second problem by using the RERDSZ field passed from the caller, which defines the size of the error data field. RERDSZ is used with the SUBST opcode to set RERDTA to the correct length (memory could be corrupted in the calling program without this step).

Chapter 3

Gracefully Handling Unexpected Errors

It's easy to write defensive RPG for errors you can anticpate, but you need this routine so your programs behave gracefully when unexpected errors occur and to make your RPG more robust and predictable.

The best defense against program errors is to predict and code for specific error possibilities in your RPG code. With careful planning and thought, you can write nearly bulletproof RPG programs without needing a generic error handler (i.e., code defensively against array index errors or attempts to divide by zero). However, there are times when an error occurs that you simply didn't anticpate. Your RPG should be robust enough to gracefully intercept these annoying errors and provide the investigative information you need to understand the cause and to help you avoid them in the future.

This chapter includes the code you need to provide your RPG with an effective and robust unexpected error handler to do just that. Together with RPG's program status data structure and RPG's program exception/error subroutine, *PSSR, this chapter's code will give you all the unexpected error protection you need (see Chapter 2 for more information about the program-status data structure). With this code in place, when an unexpected error occurs, the user is shown an informational screen with detailed error information; the system operator is notified that an error has occurred; a job log is printed; and a formatted RPG dump is performed. And after all that error reporting is completed, the offending RPG program ends.

To use this code in your programs, perform the following two tasks once:

- Create display file PSSRD with the DDS shown in Figure 3.1.
- Compile the CL program PSSRC with the code shown in Figure 3.2.

FIGURE 3.1
DDS Used by CL Program PSSRC

```
... 1 ...+... 2 ...+... 3 ...+... 4 ...+... 5 ...+... 6 ...+... 7 ...+... 8
 *-------------------------------------------------------------------
 * PSSRD - Display file for CL program PSSRD
 *-------------------------------------------------------------------
A                                      DSPSIZ(24 80 *DS3)
A          R RECORD
A                              1 34'Program Error'
A                                DSPATR(HI)
```

continued

FIGURE 3.1 *CONTINUED*

```
... 1 ...+... 2 ...+... 3 ...+... 4 ...+... 5 ...+... 6 ...+... 7 ...+... 8
A                                         3 2'This program has detected an error-
A                                           from which it cannot recover.'
A                                           COLOR(BLU)
A                                         4 2'The System Operator has been notif-
A                                           ied.'
A                                           COLOR(BLU)
A                                         5 2'Press Enter to cancel this program-
A                                           .'
A                                           COLOR(BLU)
A                                         6 2'The Data Processing Department wil-
A                                           l contact you with instructions.'
A                                           COLOR(BLU)
A                                         8 2'Job name . . . . :'
A            SDSJOB       10    0  8 23
A                                         9 2'User profile . . :'
A            SDSUSR       10    0  9 23
A                                        10 2'Job number . . . :'
A            SDSNBR        6    0 10 23
A                                        12 2'Program  . . . . :'
A            SDSPGM       10    0 12 23
A                                        13 2'Status code  . . :'
A            SDSSTS        5    0 13 23
A                                        14 2'Statement number :'
A            SDSSEQ        7    0 14 23
A                                        15 2'Error message  . :'
A            SDSERR        7    0 15 23
A                                        16 2'Message text . . :'
A            SDSMSG       80    0 16 23
A                                        23 2'Press Enter to continue.'
```

FIGURE 3.2

CL Program to Convey Error to User

```
/*
 |  ----------------------------------------------------------- +
 |  PSSRC CL program to post a message to a user and print      +
 |  job log when a program ends abnormally.                     +
 |  Called from *PSSR subroutine in member PSSR.                +
 |  ----------------------------------------------------------- +
 */

PGM PARM( &SDSSTS                                               +
          &SDSPGM                                               +
          &SDSSEQ                                               +
          &SDSERR                                               +
          &SDSMSG                                               +
          &SDSJOB                                               +
          &SDSUSR                                               +
          &SDSNBR )                                             +

DCL     &SDSSTS   *CHAR    5
DCL     &SDSPGM   *CHAR   10
DCL     &SDSSEQ   *CHAR    7
DCL     &SDSERR   *CHAR    7
DCL     &SDSMSG   *CHAR   80
DCL     &SDSJOB   *CHAR   10
DCL     &SDSUSR   *CHAR   10
DCL     &SDSNBR   *CHAR    6
```

continued

FIGURE 3.2 *CONTINUED*

```
DCLF       FILE( PSSRD )
SNDMSG     MSG( 'Job'   *BCAT  &SDSNBR *TCAT '/'      *TCAT  +
                 &SDSUSR *TCAT  '/'     *TCAT &SDSJOB *BCAT  +
                 'has encountered an error with program'    +
                 *BCAT   &SDSPGM       *TCAT              +
                 '. Examine RPG dump and job log.' )        +
           TOUSR( *SYSOPR )                                 +
           MSGTYPE( *INQ )
SNDRCVF

DSPJOBLOG  OUTPUT( *PRINT )

ENDPGM
```

After creating these two objects, make sure they are available in a library in your AS/400's library list. Then, in any RPG program that you want to protect against unexpected errors:

- Include the /COPY statement for the CTLWDMP module (Figure 3.3) as the first line in your program (or, alternatively, ensure that column 15 of your program's H-spec has a 1 in column 15 — this entry is required to ensure a formatted RPG dump).

- Include the /COPY statement for the PGMSDS module (Figure 2.1 from Chapter 2) in the I-spec area of your RPG program.

- Include the /COPY statement for the PSSR module (Figure 3.4) in the subroutine area of your RPG program.

FIGURE 3.3
RPG H-Spec with DEBUG On

```
... 1 ...+... 2 ...+... 3 ...+... 4 ...+... 5 ...+... 6 ...+... 7 ...+... 8
*-----------------------------------------------------------------------
* CTLWDMP - Program control spec with DUMP specified for a
*           formatted RPG dump.
*
* This H-spec is required by the *PSSR
* subroutine in member PSSR to create a formatted RPG dump
* when an abnormal program end occurs.
*-----------------------------------------------------------------------
*
H       1
```

Figure 3.4
PSSR Subroutine Module

```
... 1 ...+... 2 ...+... 3 ...+... 4 ...+... 5 ...+... 6 ...+... 7 ...+... 8
 *-----------------------------------------------------------------
 * PSSR  - Program exception/error subroutine
 *
 * Requires copy modules:
 *   CTLWDMP  - Program header with a '1' in column 15

    *   PGMSDS   - Program status data structure
 *
 * Returns:
 *   Ends program and posts message to user and to job log.
 *-----------------------------------------------------------------
C            *PSSR      BEGSR
C                       CALL 'PSSRC'                    99
C                       PARM           PSSTS
C                       PARM           PSPGM
C                       PARM           PSSEQ
C                       PARM           PSMSID
C                       PARM           PSDTA
C                       PARM           PSJOB
C                       PARM           PSUSR
C                       PARM           PSJOBN
C                       DUMP
C                       ENDSR'*CANCL'
```

With this approach, the following snippet of code will perform graceful error handling when divide-by-zero is attempted:

```
/COPY CTLWDMP
/COPY PGMSDS
 *
C                       Z-ADD0         DIVISR  30
C            25         DIV  DIVISR    RESULT  30
C                       MOVE *ON       *INLR
 *
/COPY PSSR
```

Chapter 4

Using the File Information Data Structure

File information data structures provide your RPG programs with useful exception, error-handling, and hard-to-get runtime information about disk and printer files.

You can define a file information data structure (INFDS) for each file to make file exception/error information available to your RPG programs. Each file can have an associated file information data structure, but each file's structure must be unique to that file (i.e., an INFDS cannot be shared between two files). Some of the information provided in a file's INFDS is useful for debugging or testing purposes. For example, a status code is available (positions 11–15) to indicate the status of the last file operation performed. In addition to debugging or testing, your program may need INFDS information for runtime application purposes. For example, the current print line (positions 367–368) is tracked for printer files (if you need to manually track overflow), and you can also use the INFDS to determine the record length of a disk file. In addition, an INFDS can tell you the name of a file as it is specified on the F-spec (in positions 1–8) and the actual name of the file, which would be different from the F-spec name if a file override is being used (in positions 83–92).

Member FINFDS (Figure 4.1) contains the RPG module required to "snap" in a file information data structure for a file.

FIGURE 4.1

File Feedback Module INFDS for Disk and Printer Files

```
... 1 ...+... 2 ...+... 3 ...+... 4 ...+... 5 ...+... 6 ...+... 7 ...+... 8
*-----------------------------------------------------------------------
* FINFDS - File information feedback data structure
*
* Function:
*   Defines disk and printer file feedback area.
*
*  FINFDS - file_inf_DS
*    FIFPN    file_name (from program)
*    FIOPN    file_open
*    FIEOF    file_eof
*    FISTS    file_sts
*    FIOPCD   file_opcode
*    FIRTNN   file_rpg_routine
*    FISTN    file_src_nbr
```

continued

FIGURE 4.1 *CONTINUED*

```
 ... 1 ...+... 2 ...+... 3 ...+... 4 ...+... 5 ...+... 6 ...+... 7 ...+... 8
  *     FIRCDN    file_rcd_name
  *     FIMGID    file_msg_id
  *     FIODP     file_odp
  *     FIFINA    file_name_actual
  *     FILINA    file_lib_name
  *     FISPNA    file_splf_name
  *     FISLNA    file_splf_lib
  *     FISPLN    file_splf_nbr
  *     FIRECL    file_recl
  *     FIMBRN    file_mbr_name
  *     FIFTYP    file_type
  *     FIROWS    file_rows
  *     FICOLS    file_cols
  *     FIRECS    file_recs_at_open
  *     FIATYP    file_access_type
  *     FIDUPK    file_dupe_key
  *     FISRCF    file_src_ind
  *     FIOFLN    file_of_line_nbr
  *     FIFMTN    file_last_format
  *     FIRLEN    file_recl_pro
  *     FILNNO    file_line_nbr
  *     FIPGCT    file_page_cnt
  *     FIKEYF    file_nbr_keys
  *     FIKEYL    file_key_len
  *     FIMBRN    file_mbr_nbr
  *     FIRRN     file_rrn
  *     FIKEYV    file_key_val
  *------------------------------------------------------------------------
IFINFDS         DS                             512
I                                        1    8 FIFPN
I                                        9    9 FIOPN
I                                       10   10 FIEOF
I                                       11  150FISTS
I                                       16   21 FIOPCD
I                                       22   29 FIRTNN
I                                       30   37 FISTN
I                                       38   45 FIRCDN
I                                       46   52 FIMGID
I                                       81   82 FIODP
I                                       83   92 FIFINA
I                                       93  102 FILINA
I                                      103  112 FISPNA
I                                      113  122 FISLNA
I                                    B 123 1240FISPLN
I                                    B 125 1260FIRECL
I                                      129  138 FIMBRN
I                                    B 147 1480FIFTYP
I                                    B 152 1530FIROWS
I                                    B 154 1550FICOLS
I                                    B 156 1590FIRECS
I                                      160  161 FIATYP
I                                      162  162 FIDUPK
I                                      163  163 FISRCF
I                                      188  189 FIOFLN
I                                      261  270 FIFMTN
I                                    B 283 2860FIRLEN
I                                    B 367 3680FILNNO
I                                    B 369 3720FIPGCT
I                                    B 387 3880FIKEYF
I                                    B 393 3940FIKEYL
I                                    B 395 3960FIMBRN
I                                    B 397 4000FIRRN
I                                      401  499 FIKEYV
```

As you can see, lots of handy data is available in an INFDS. (In the next chapter, we'll provide an abbreviated INFDS for workstation files, which is handy for cursor management and subfile relative record number tracking.) Note that our INFDS member doesn't contain all the subfields available for a disk or printer file, but it does contain the most commonly used subfields. If you have a special use that requires subfields we haven't provided, simply add them to the FINFDS module. See the *RPG Reference Manual* (SC09-1817) and the *Data Management Guide* (SC41-3710) for detailed information about all the subfields available in the file information data structures.

To provide an INFDS for any file in your RPG programs:

- Include the /COPY statement for the FINFDS module in the I-spec area of your RPG program.

- For every file for which you need a file information data structure, code the "KINFDS" entry in positions 53–58 and the name of an associated file-specific data structure in positions 60–65 on that file's F-spec.

- In the I-spec area, code a data structure I-spec for each data stucture you named in the previous step. Make sure that the name specified in positions 7–12 matches the name supplied in the F-spec in columns 60–65. Also, be sure to code these file information data structures with a 512-byte length.

The sample code below shows a snippet of RPG that provides two file information data structures, one for a disk file and one for a printer file. After each file operation, you can move one of these data structures into the FINFDS data structure (specified in the FINFDS /COPY module) to make the data structure's subfields available to your RPG program. Note the technique here of specifying a data structure length of 512 on both the FINFDS data structure in the /COPY module and in each file-specific data structure you need. This makes it easy to move the contents of one data structure to another (i.e., it makes it easy to map the information in a 512-byte block of file-specific data to the subfields defined in FINFDS). With this technique, no subfields are needed in the file-specific data structures you provide.

```
FMYFILE   IF  E                        DISK        KINFDS MYIFDS
FQSYSPRT  O   F    132                 PRINTER     KINFDS QSIFDS
 *
 /COPY FINFDS
IMYIFDS      IDS                                512
IQSIFDS      IDS                                512
    :
    :
 * After a file operation to MYFILE, make its
 * file information data structure available.
C                      MOVELMYIFDS    FINFDS
 *
 * After a file operation to QSYSPRT, make its
 * file information data structure available.
C                      MOVELQSIFDS    FINFD
```

Chapter 5

Declaring Data Types

Make your code more bulletproof and easier to troubleshoot by declaring variables to be of standard "types."

Quick, what is the fatal error in the following RPG snippet?

```
C                       Z-ADD1         X        10
C            X          DOWLE10
C                         .
C                         . Some code
C                         .
C                       ADD  1         X
C                       ENDDO
```

Something is very wrong here. Did you find the error? Here's a hint: How many times will the loop above be executed?

The code implies 10, doesn't it? But the correct answer isn't 10. This RPG code will cause an infinite loop, continually executing the code within the body of the loop. Why? Because the variable X has been declared as a 1-digit variable. When X's value is nine, and one is added to it, its new value becomes not 10, as desired, but rather zero! This error could have been avoided if X had been declared as a 2-digit value — but then pity the poor maintenance programmer who three years later needs to change the loop to perform 100 times.

A solution to arbitrarily assigning data types and data lengths is to use standard data "types." Figure 5.1 shows the STDTYPES RPG member, which declares five data types: Boolean, character, integer, long integer, and message ID.

FIGURE 5.1
STDTYPES Standard Data Type Declarations

```
... 1 ...+... 2 ...+... 3 ...+... 4 ...+... 5 ...+... 6 ...+... 7 ...+... 8
*-----------------------------------------------------------------------
* STDTYPES - Standard program data type declarations.
*
* Function:
*   Defines standard data type templates.
*
*   #BOOL  - Boolean
*   #CHAR  - Character
*   #INT   - Integer
*   #LINT  - Long integer
*   #MSGID - Message id
*-----------------------------------------------------------------------
```

continued

FIGURE 5.1 *CONTINUED*

```
... 1 ...+... 2 ...+... 3 ...+... 4 ...+... 5 ...+... 6 ...+... 7 ...+... 8
I          IDS
I                                          1   1 #BOOL
I                                          2   2 #CHAR
I                                          3  70#INT
I                                          8 220#LINT
```

To use this member, simply copy it into your RPG program's I-specs with /COPY and then declare variables as needed with the DEFN operation code, as shown in the following example. In this example, X is declared as an integer, COUNT is declared as a long integer, CUSTYP is declared as a character, and MSGID is declared as a message ID. It's probably best to put the like defines in the *INSR subroutine.

```
I/COPY STDTYPES
   :
C          *LIKE     DEFN #INT     X
C          *LIKE     DEFN #LINT    COUNT
C          *LIKE     DEFN #CHAR    CUSTYP
C          *LIKE     DEFN #MSG     MSGID
```

Note that the integer data type, as defined in STDTYPES, provides an integer value with up to five digits. Thus, there is some possibility of overflowing even that value in a loop counter; but it isn't very likely. If you're not sure whether the 5-digit integer type is long enough, use the long integer type.

We normally place /COPY members in a source file named QRPGSRC in a copy book library. Putting this library in the library list makes the included members available without needing to hard-code the library and source file name in the /COPY statement. This makes it easy to change the name of the copy book library in the library list, and test or use different versions of the includes. The /COPY examples shown in this book never include library or source file names.

Chapter 6

Mapping Externally Described Fields to Array Elements

Overcome an annoying constraint of RPG's externally described files with this field-to-array mapping technique.

RPG/400's externally described files offer many advantages over program-described files, especially in terms of ensuring reliability and consistency. There are, however, a few annoyances associated with externally described files. Specifically, you may find it challenging to effectively map fields in an externally described file to array elements. So in this chapter, we provide a technique that maps fields in an externally described record to an array. Our example shows that the fields being mapped are stored contiguously in the file, but the technique would also work for noncontiguous fields.

Consider the LEDGER file described by the DDS shown in Figure 6.1.

FIGURE 6.1
LEDGER File DDS

```
... 1 ...+... 2 ...+... 3 ...+... 4 ...+... 5 ...+... 6 ...+... 7 ...+... 8
A                                        UNIQUE
A           R LEREC
A             LESTOR        4S 0
A             LEACCT        4S 0
A             LEDEPT        1S 0
A             LELOC         2S 0
  *
A             LECODE        3A
A             LEDRCR        1A
A             LENAME       24A
  *
A             LECBEG        9P 2
  *
A             LECJAN        9P 2
A             LECFEB        9P 2
A             LECMAR        9P 2
A             LECAPR        9P 2
A             LECMAY        9P 2
A             LECJUN        9P 2
A             LECJUL        9P 2
A             LECAUG        9P 2
A             LECSEP        9P 2
A             LECOCT        9P 2
A             LECNOV        9P 2
A             LECDEC        9P 2
  *
A           K LESTOR
A           K LEACCT
A           K LEDEPT
A           K LELOC
```

This is a general ledger master file; its records contain summary information about general ledger accounts. Included in this information is a group of 12 contiguous fields (LECJAN through LECDEC) that represent monthly balances for an account.

In many RPG programs, it would be far handier to deal with these contiguous monthly balance fields as elements of an array rather than dealing with them directly by explicit field name. For example, consider summing monthly balances up to and including a given month (e.g., when you need to calculate the ending balance through May to print a May financial statement). Using an array, where the field ENDMON is the ending month number, the following four lines of code are all that you need to calculate any given month's ending balance:

```
C                           Z-ADDØ          ENDBAL
C              1            DO    ENDMON     X
C              CUR,X        ADD   ENDBAL
C                           ENDDO
```

This coding would be far more complex if it were done by referencing the individual field names of each of the 12 monthly balances. Thus, the challenge is to effectively map the externally described fields to array elements.

You can use several techniques to map the field names to array element names, including using external data structures and hard-coding overlapping fields with program-described data structures. These methods, though, are error-prone because of their high sensitivity to field positions in the file. The most straightforward and easy-to-maintain method for mapping the field names to array element names is to simply use the RPG I-spec field-renaming facility to rename the externally described field names to array element names.

For example, the code below maps the 12 monthly balance fields in the LEDGER file to array elements of the CUR array:

```
FLEDGER  IP  E                    DISK
 *
E                      CUR        12 9 2
 *
ILEREC
I              LECJAN                        CUR,1
I              LECFEB                        CUR,2
I              LECMAR                        CUR,3
I              LECAPR                        CUR,4
I              LECMAY                        CUR,5
I              LECJUN                        CUR,6
I              LECJUL                        CUR,7
I              LECAUG                        CUR,8
I              LECSEP                        CUR,9
I              LECOCT                        CUR,1Ø
I              LECNOV                        CUR,11
I              LECDEC                        CUR,12
```

RPG's I-spec renaming facility makes the original field name (e.g., LECJAN) unavailable to your RPG program. If you need to reference an array element value in DDS (for printer or display files), you'll need to assign fields to an RPG program for that purpose. For example, if your DDS uses the field name MBJAN to display the LECJAN field (which has now been mapped to the CUR,1 array element), simply insert Z-ADD CUR,1 to MBJAN before your program writes the display file format, as follows:

```
C                        Z-ADDCUR,1    MBJAN
```

This renaming method is superior to other field-to-array mapping techniques because it is less dependent on physical field positions to work — the code to rename the fields doesn't require a knowledge of field beginning or ending positions. The I-specs used to rename the fields are completely independent of field positions in the file. Be aware, though, that the array declaration is dependent on the file layout — if the LEDGER file were changed to make all 12 monthly balance fields 10 bytes long instead of 9 bytes long, the mapping would fail if the CUR array definition was not changed.

To simplify coding changes across many programs, consider creating external modules that declare the target array and that rename the LEDGER file fields (as shown in Figures 6.2 and 6.3).

FIGURE 6.2
Member LECARR, Which Maps LEDGER File Monthly Balances to Elements of the CUR Array

```
... 1 ...+... 2 ...+... 3 ...+... 4 ...+... 5 ...+... 6 ...+... 7 ...+... 8
 * Rename LEDGER file monthly balances to CUR array elements.
 * Requires that member
ILEREC
I              LECJAN                      CUR,1
I              LECFEB                      CUR,2
I              LECMAR                      CUR,3
I              LECAPR                      CUR,4
I              LECMAY                      CUR,5
I              LECJUN                      CUR,6
I              LECJUL                      CUR,7
I              LECAUG                      CUR,8
I              LECSEP                      CUR,9
I              LECOCT                      CUR,10
I              LECNOV                      CUR,11
I              LECDEC                      CUR,1
```

FIGURE 6.3
Member GLARR, Which Declares CUR Array to Hold LEDGER File Monthly Balances

```
... 1 ...+... 2 ...+... 3 ...+... 4 ...+... 5 ...+... 6 ...+... 7 ...+... 8
 * Twelve-element array to hold GL monthly balances
E                   CUR        12   9 2
```

By isolating this code in these modules, you would only have one place to maintain each definition should the layout of the LEDGER file ever change. Using these modules reduces the coding necessary to map the fields to array elements. The GLARR member goes anywhere in the RPG program's E-specs and the LECARR member goes anywhere in the RPG program's I-specs, as shown in the code snippet below:

```
FLEDGER  IP  E                      DISK
 *
 /COPY GLARR
E... other E-specs as necessary
 *
I... other I-specs as necessary
I...
 /COPY LECARR
```

Chapter 7

Sorting Arrays

Replace RPG's SORTA op-code with the templates in this chapter for a more flexible way to sort arrays.

It's a simple fact of life: The more you have, the more you want. RPG's sort array (SORTA) opcode is a typical example of this maxim. At first, the capability to sort a whole array in ascending order appears to satisfy every need. Then you start hitting the quirky programs: In one you need to sort the front end of an array, leaving the blank elements at the end; in another you need to sort an array in descending order. The two templates in this chapter provide different approaches to solving both these problems. You won't need these templates every day, but it's handy to know you have them in reserve for when the occasion arises.

In this chapter we use templates, not /COPY modules. A template is a generic member you copy into a source program using SEU and then modify to fit the program's specific requirements. We use templates because every array is unique. To manipulate an array, you must work with the actual array — you can't just copy it to an all-purpose array and then execute some generic function. The templates included in this chapter are

ARYSRT   provides a simple way to sort small arrays of up to approximately 200 elements (Figure 7.1)

ARYQSRT   provides a complex way to sort arrays of any size very quickly (Figure 7.2)

FIGURE 7.1
ARYSRT Sort Array Template

```
... 1 ...+... 2 ...+... 3 ...+... 4 ...+... 5 ...+... 6 ...+... 7 ...+... 8
*-----------------------------------------------------------------------
* ARYSRT    Sort array template
*
* Function:
*   Sorts an array between the specified bottom and top
*   entries in either ascending or descending order.
*
* Usage:
*   Copy this template into your program and replace all
*   &values listed below with your actual program variables.
*   Syntax errors will occur if the array name is not 3
*   characters long.
*
* Expects:
*   &ar   -   array
*   &len  -   entry_len (with decimal places if numeric)
```

continued

FIGURE 7.1 CONTINUED

```
... 1 ...+... 2 ...+... 3 ...+... 4 ...+... 5 ...+... 6 ...+... 7 ...+... 8
*   &temp   - temp_entry
*   &bot    - bot_index (first entry to sort)
*   &top    - top_index (last entry to sort)
*   ARYDSC - array_descending (optional)
*
* Returns:
*   ARYERR   array_error *OFF
*---------------------------------------------------------------------------
C           &arSRT    BEGSR
*
* Declare variables
*
C                     Z-ADD@I       @I      50
C                     Z-ADD@O       @O      50
C                     Z-ADD@NEXT    @NEXT   50
C                     Z-ADD&BOT     @BOT    50
C                     Z-ADD&TOP     @TOP    50
C                     MOVE &temp    &temp &len
C                     MOVE *OFF     ARYERR  1
C                     MOVE ARYDSC   ARYDSC  1
*
* For first to last but one element
*
C           &top      SUB  1        @TOP
C           &bot      DO   @TOP      @O
*
* .Compare with unsorted elements
*
C           @O        ADD  1        @NEXT
C           @NEXT     DO   &top      @I
*
* ..Swap out of sequence elements
*
C           ARYDSC    IFNE *ON
*
C           &ar,@I    IFLT &ar,@O
C                     MOVE &ar,@O   &temp
C                     MOVE &ar,@I   &ar,@O
C                     MOVE &temp    &ar,@I
C                     ENDIF
*
C                     ELSE
*
C           &ar,@I    IFGT &ar,@O
C                     MOVE &ar,@O   &temp
C                     MOVE &ar,@I   &ar,@O
C                     MOVE &temp    &ar,@I
C                     ENDIF
*
C                     ENDIF
*
C                     ENDDO
*
C                     ENDDO
*
* Clear optional arguments
*
C                     MOVE *OFF     ARYDSC
*
C                     ENDSR
```

FIGURE 7.2
ARYQSRT Quicksort Array Template

```
... 1 ...+... 2 ...+... 3 ...+... 4 ...+... 5 ...+... 6 ...+... 7 ...+... 8
*-----------------------------------------------------------------------
* ARYQSRT   Quicksort array template
*
* Function:
*   Very quickly sorts an array between the specified bottom
*   and top entries in either ascending or descending order.
*
* Usage:
*   Copy this template into your program and replace all
*   &values listed below with your actual program variables.
*   Syntax errors will occur if the array name is not
*   three characters long.
*
* Expects:
*   &ar    - array
*   &len   - entry_len (with decimal places if numeric)
*   &pivot - pivot_entry
*   &temp  - temp_entry
*   &bot   - bot_index (first entry to sort)
*   &top   - top_index (last entry to sort)
*   ARYDSC - array_descending (optional)
*
* Returns:
*   ARYERR - array_error on stack overflow (can't happen!)
*
*-----------------------------------------------------------------------
C           &arSRT     BEGSR
*
* Declare variables
*
C                      Z-ADD0       @ARLVL  30
C                      MOVE @ARSTK   @ARSTK250
C                      MOVE @ARSHF   @ARSHF240
C                      MOVE @ARTOP   @ARTOP 10
C                      Z-ADD25      @ARMAX  50
C                      Z-ADD@L      @L      50
C                      Z-ADD@M      @M      50
C                      Z-ADD@R      @R      50
C                      Z-ADD&bot    @BOT    50
C                      Z-ADD&top    @TOP    50
C                      MOVE &pivot  &pivot&len
C                      MOVE &temp   &temp &len
C                      MOVE *OFF    ARYERR   1
C                      MOVE ARYDSC  ARYDSC   1
*
* Sort the array
*
C           *ON        DOWEQ*ON
*
C                      SELEC
*
* .Something to sort in subset
*
C           @BOT       WHLT @TOP
*
```

continued

FIGURE 7.2 *CONTINUED*

```
... 1 ...+... 2 ...+... 3 ...+... 4 ...+... 5 ...+... 6 ...+... 7 ...+... 8
C                     Z-ADD@BOT      @L
C                     Z-ADD@TOP      @R
 *
 * ..Get pivot from middle of subset
 *
C           @TOP      SUB  @BOT      @M
C                     MULT 0.5       @M
C                     ADD  @BOT      @M
C                     MOVE &ar,@M    &pivot
 *
 * ..Partition the subset into two new subsets about the pivot:
 *    left subset <= pivot <= right subset
 *   (If descending array, reverse the order)
 *
C           @L        DOWLE@R
 *
 * ...Advance left and right pointers while elements in sequence
 *
C           ARYDSC    IFNE *ON
 *
C           &ar,@L    DOWLT&pivot
C                     ADD  1         @L
C                     ENDDO
C           &ar,@R    DOWGT&pivot
C                     SUB  1         @R
C                     ENDDO
 *
C                     ELSE
 *
C           &ar,@L    DOWGT&pivot
C                     ADD  1         @L
C                     ENDDO
C           &ar,@R    DOWLT&pivot
C                     SUB  1         @R
C                     ENDDO
 *
C                     ENDIF
 *
 * ...Swap out of sequence elements
 *
C                     SELEC
C           @L        WHLT @R
C                     MOVE &ar,@L    &temp
C                     MOVE &ar,@R    &ar,@L
C                     MOVE &temp     &ar,@R
C                     ADD  1         @L
C                     SUB  1         @R
C           @L        WHEQ @R
C                     ADD  1         @L
C                     SUB  1         @R
C                     ENDSL
 *
C                     ENDDO
 *
 * ..Find subset with fewest entries for next pass:
 *    If right subset, save right and use left on next pass
 *    If left subset, save left and use right on next pass
 *
C           @R        IFGE @M
C                     MOVEL@L        @ARTOP
```

continued

FIGURE 7.2 CONTINUED

```
... 1 ...+... 2 ...+... 3 ...+... 4 ...+... 5 ...+... 6 ...+... 7 ...+... 8
C                       MOVE @TOP      @ARTOP
C                       Z-ADD@BOT      @BOT
C                       Z-ADD@R        @TOP
C                       ELSE
C                       MOVEL@BOT      @ARTOP
C                       MOVE @R        @ARTOP
C                       Z-ADD@L        @BOT
C                       Z-ADD@TOP      @TOP
C                       ENDIF
 *
 * ..Push saved subset onto stack, or exit on overflow
 *
C           @ARLVL      IFLT @ARMAX
C                       ADD  1         @ARLVL
C                       MOVEL@ARSTK    @ARSHF
C                       MOVE @ARSHF    @ARSTK
C                       MOVEL@ARTOP    @ARSTK
C                       ELSE
C                       MOVE *ON       ARYERR
C                       LEAVE
C                       ENDIF
 *
 * .Something to pop from stack
 *
C           @ARLVL      WHGT 0
 *
C                       MOVEL@ARTOP    @BOT
C                       MOVE @ARTOP    @TOP
 *
C                       SUB  1         @ARLVL
C                       MOVE @ARSTK    @ARSHF
C                       MOVEL@ARSHF    @ARSTK
C                       MOVEL@ARSTK    @ARTOP
 *
 * .Sort completed
 *
C                       OTHER
 *
C                       LEAVE
 *
C                       ENDSL
 *
C                       ENDDO
 *
 * Clear optional arguments
 *
C                       MOVE *OFF      ARYDSC
 *
C                       ENDSR
```

Both templates provide exactly the same functionality; the only difference is performance. The time required to run ARYSRT increases exponentially with the size of the array, whereas ARYQSRT exhibits the same performance characteristics as the SORTA opcode, with the sort time increasing logarithmically with the size of the array. Because both templates are very simple to incorporate into your programs, we recommend you use ARYQSRT. Although ARYQSRT contains more code, it only requires one additional substitution, making it almost as easy to "plug in" as ARYSRT is.

Let's look at a simple example of how to use the templates. Suppose you are writing a program to validate the class of an item. Because class validation occurs often in this program, and because the ITMCLS file is a known, relatively static size, it makes sense to store the item classes in an array for fast access:

```
*
* Item class file
FITMCLS  IF  E                       DISK
*
* Item class array
E                   CLS      200  4
*
* Size of item class array
I              200                 C           CLSSIZ
*
* Load item class array
C                        Z-ADD0      C        50
C                        READ ITMCLS                    99
C            *IN99       DOWEQ*OFF
C                        ADD  1      C
C                        MOVE ICCLS  CLS,C
C                        READ ITMCLS                    99
C                        ENDDO
```

The CLSSIZ named constant defines the declared size of the CLS array. The C field is used as an index to the array, and after the DOWEQ loop, contains the actual number of elements in the array.

Then you add the code to sort the array using the ARYSRT template in three simple steps. First, you key the code to execute the sort function:

```
*
* Sort only filled elements of item class array.
C                        Z-ADD1      CLSBOT  50
C                        Z-ADDC      CLSTOP  50
C                        EXSR CLSSRT
```

where CLSBOT and CLSTOP define the actual bottom and top entries used in the array, and the subroutine name consists of the array name followed by SRT. When subroutine CLSSRT is executed, it only sorts the CLS array from the elements at CLSBOT to CLSTOP, leaving any blank elements beyond CLSTOP at the end of the array. If you want to include blank elements in the sort and move them to the front of the array, you set CLSTOP to the declared size of the array in CLSSIZ before executing CLSSRT, as shown below:

```
*
* Sort all elements of item class array.
C                        Z-ADD1        CLSBOT  50
C                        Z-ADDCLSSIZ   CLSTOP  50
C                        EXSR CLSSRT
```

Next, you copy the ARYSRT template (Figure 7.1) into the source program t the end of the C-specs. Finally, you execute the following change commands on the SEU command line to replace the generic values in the template with the specific values for the item class array:

```
C    &ar       CLS       A
C    &len      ' 4 '     A
C    &temp     CLSTMP    A
C    &bot      CLSBOT    A
C    &top      CLSTOP    A
```

&ar is replaced by the array name CLS, and creates a subroutine name of CLSSRT. Please note that the array name must be 3 characters long; otherwise, code can be shifted to the left or right, resulting in syntax errors. &len is replaced by both the length of an element and its number of decimal places, as used in columns 49–52 of a C-spec. &temp is replaced by the name of a work variable used to store an element from the array. &bot and &top are replaced by the CLSBOT and CLSTOP fields mentioned above.

To use the ARYQSRT template (Figure 7.2) instead of ARYSRT, you follow the steps described above and execute one additional change command on the SEU command line:

```
C    &pivot   CLSPVT   A
```

&pivot is replaced by the name of a work variable used to store an element from the array.

By default, both templates sort an array in ascending order. However, the sort templates include a Boolean flag named ARYDSC which, when set to *ON, overrides the default behavior of the sort routines. To sort an array in descending order, you simply set field ARYDSC on before executing the sort subroutine:

```
*
* Sort item class array in descending order
C                    Z-ADD1       CLSBOT   50
C                    Z-ADDC       CLSTOP   50
C                    MOVE *ON     ARYDSC
C                    EXSR CLSSRT
```

The sort templates in this chapter show how you can improve upon the standard functionality in RPG/400. With the right algorithm, as shown by ARYQSRT, you can also achieve this without loss of performance. As well as being useful for sorting arrays, the templates can serve as blueprints for sorting other storage areas, such as multiple-occurrence data structures or user spaces. The next chapter shows how, in conjunction with these sort routines, you can code a speedy, more functional replacement for RPG's LOKUP opcode.

Chapter 8

Searching Arrays

Replace RPG's LOKUP opcode with the template in this chapter for a better and faster way to search arrays.

RPG's LOKUP opcode is notoriously slow with large arrays, and it can be a real resource hog when used frequently. To go with the sort techniques in the last chapter, we've written an RPG template, ARYSCH, which you can use instead of LOKUP. ARYSCH binary search is not only faster than LOKUP for large arrays, but ARYSCH also offers some additional functionality. With ARYSCH, you can limit the search to part of an array, search arrays in ascending or descending order, search for a partial match, and find the nearest element to the search argument when an exact match can't be found.

In the previous chapter, we showed you how to load and sort an array of item classes, CLS. We used two pointers to define the bottom and top of the data in the array, stored in the fields CLSBOT and CLSTOP. Now that the array is sorted, we can use the ARYSCH template to find any element in the array. First, you key the code to execute the search function:

```
     * Set value to search for in code somewhere
    C                     MOVE '23'      ICCLS    P
     *
     * Search array for item class value in ICCLS field
     * and save index in C
    C                     MOVE ICCLS     CLSARG
    C                     EXSR CLSSCH
    C                     Z-ADDARYIDX    C
    C         ARYERR      IFEQ *OFF
      :                   .code for exact match
    C                     ELSE
      :                   .code for nearest entry

    C                     ENDIF
```

In this case, the CLSSCH search subroutine will attempt to find the item class value of 23. It will search and return either the index of the matching element in ARYIDX with ARYERR set off, or the index of the nearest element in ARYIDX with ARYERR set on.

Next, you copy the SCHARY template (Figure 8.1) into the source program at the end of the C-specs.

FIGURE 8.1
ARYSCH Search Array Template

```
... 1 ...+... 2 ...+... 3 ...+... 4 ...+... 5 ...+... 6 ...+... 7 ...+... 8
*-------------------------------------------------------------------------
* ARYSCH   Binary search array template
*
* Function:
*   Search an array between the specified bottom and top
*   entries for a value. The array may be in either ascending
*   or descending sequence.
*
* Usage:
*   Copy this template into your program and replace all
*   &values listed below with your actual program variables.
*   Syntax errors will occur if the array name is not
*   three characters long.
*
* Expects:
*   &ar    - array (in ascending or descending order)
*   &len   - arg_len (with decimal places if numeric)
*   &arg   - search_arg
*   &comp  - compare_val
*   &bot   - bot_index (first entry to search)
*   &top   - top_index (last entry to search)
*   ARYDSC - array_descending (optional)
*
* Returns:
*   ARYIDX - array_index of nearest element
*   ARYERR - array_error if not exact match
*-------------------------------------------------------------------------
C           &arSCH     BEGSR
*
* Declare variables
*
C                      Z-ADD0          ARYIDX  50
C                      Z-ADD&bot       @BOT    50
C                      Z-ADD&top       @TOP    50
C                      Z-ADD0          @MID    50
C                      MOVE &arg       &arg  &len
C                      MOVE &comp      &comp &len
C                      MOVE ARYDSC     ARYDSC  1
C                      MOVE *ON        ARYERR  1
*
* Search array between subset of bottom to top
*
C           @BOT       DOWLE@TOP
*
* .Get compare value from middle of subset
*
C           @TOP       SUB @BOT        @MID
C                      MULT 0.5        @MID
C                      ADD @BOT        @MID
C                      MOVEL&ar,@MID   &comp
*
* .Compare middle value to argument:
*    If less, use top half of subset on next pass
*    If greater, use bottom half of subset on next pass
*    Else equal, search complete
* (If descending array, reverse the order)
*
C           ARYDSC     IFNE *ON
*
```

continued

```
... 1 ...+... 2 ...+... 3 ...+... 4 ...+... 5 ...+... 6 ...+... 7 ...+... 8
C                           SELEC
C             &comp         WHLT &arg
C             @MID          ADD  1        @BOT
C             &comp         WHGT &arg
C             @MID          SUB  1        @TOP
C                           OTHER
C                           MOVE *OFF     ARYERR
C                           LEAVE
C                           ENDSL
 *
C                           ELSE
 *
C                           SELEC
C             &comp         WHLT &arg
C             @MID          SUB  1        @TOP
C             &comp         WHGT &arg
C             @MID          ADD  1        @BOT
C                           OTHER
C                           MOVE *OFF     ARYERR
C                           LEAVE
C                           ENDSL
 *
C                           ENDIF
 *
C                           ENDDO
 *
 * Return index of nearest element
 *
C                           Z-ADD@MID     ARYIDX
 *
 * Clear optional arguments
 *
C                           MOVE *OFF     ARYDSC
 *
C                           ENDSR
```

Finally, you execute the following change commands on the SEU command line to replace the generic values in the template with the specific values for the item class array:

```
C  &ar       CLS      A
C  &len     '  4 '    A
C  &arg      CLSARG   A
C  &comp     CLSCMP   A
C  &bot      CLSBOT   A
C  &top      CLSTOP   A
```

&ar is replaced by the array name CLS and creates a subroutine name of CLSSCH. As with the templates in the previous chapter, the array name must be three characters long; otherwise, code can be shifted to the left or right, resulting in syntax errors. &len is replaced by both the length of an element and its number of decimal places, as used in columns 49–52 of a C-spec. &arg is replaced by the class field CLSARG, which contains the search argument. &comp is replaced by the name of a work variable used to store an element from the array. &bot and &top are replaced by the CLSBOT and CLSTOP fields mentioned above.

By default, the ARYSCH template searches an array in ascending order. To search an array in descending order, you simply set field ARYDSC on before executing the search subroutine:

```
*
* Search array for item class in descending order
C                     MOVE ICCLS     CLSARG
C                     MOVE *ON       ARYDSC
C                     EXSR CLSSCH
C                     Z-ADDARYIDX    C
```

You should note that the ARYSCH template only works with sorted arrays, and that ARYDSC should only be specified if the array is actually sorted in descending sequence. Unpredictable results will occur if you fail to obey these guidelines.

You can modify the behavior of ARYSCH in a couple of ways to change the results it produces. First, because the ARYSCH template only searches the range of elements between ARYBOT and ARYTOP, you can adjust the values of these fields to limit the search to a subset of elements. Second, you can replace &len in the template with the first *n* characters of an element; this lets you search for a partial match rather than an exact match on the whole element. Finally, just as with the templates in the previous chapter, you can use ARYSCH as the basis for a function to search multiple-occurrence data structures or user spaces.

Chapter 9

Multidimensional Arrays

With the templates in this chapter, you can code multidimensional arrays in RPG.

As we have seen in the past couple of chapters, although RPG's built-in array-handling capabilities are limited, all you need is a little ingenuity to really make them sizzle. While most modern programming languages support at least three-dimensional arrays, RPG is still stuck in the first dimension. So in this chapter we introduce some simple templates you can use to handle two-dimensional (2D) and three-dimensional (3D) arrays:

ARYIDX2D	converts the x and y coordinates of a 2D array into a valid RPG array index (Figure 9.1)
ARYDIM2D	converts a valid RPG array index into the x and y coordinates of a 2D array (Figure 9.2)
ARYIDX3D	converts the x, y, and z coordinates of a 3D array into a valid RPG array index (Figure 9.3)
ARYDIM3D	converts a valid RPG array index into the x, y, and z coordinates of a 3D array (Figure 9.4)

FIGURE 9.1

ARYIDX2D Return Array Index to 2D Array Template

```
... 1 ...+... 2 ...+... 3 ...+... 4 ...+... 5 ...+... 6 ...+... 7 ...+... 8
 *------------------------------------------------------------------
 * ARYIDX2D   Return array index to 2D array template
 *
 * Function:
 *   Calculates the array index to a two-dimensional array
 *   from the indexes to each of the individual dimensions.
 *
 * Usage:
 *   Copy this template into your program and replace all
 *   &values listed below with your actual program variables.
 *   Syntax errors will occur if the array name is not
 *   three characters long.
 *
 * Expects:
 *   &ar    - array
 *   &dim1  - array_dim1_size
 *   &dim2  - array_dim2_size
 *   &idx1  - array_index1
 *   &idx2  - array_index2
 *
 * Returns:
 *   ARYIDX - array_index
 *   ARYERR - array_error on out of bounds index
```

continued

FIGURE 9.1 *CONTINUED*

```
... 1 ...+... 2 ...+... 3 ...+... 4 ...+... 5 ...+... 6 ...+... 7 ...+... 8
 *---------------------------------------------------------------------------
C           &arIDX       BEGSR
 *
C           @&arD1       IFEQ 0
C                        Z ADD&dim2    @&arD2 50
C           @&arD2       MULT &dim1    @&arD1 50
C                        ENDIF
 *
C           &idx1        IFLT 1
C           &idx1        ORGT &dim1
C           &idx2        ORLT 1
C           &idx2        ORGT &dim2
 *
C                        Z ADD0        ARYIDX 50
C                        MOVE *ON      ARYERR 1
 *
C                        ELSE
 *
C           &idx1        SUB  1        @&arI1 50
C                        MULT @&arD2   @&arI1
 *
C           &idx2        ADD  @&arI1   ARYIDX
C                        MOVE *OFF     ARYERR
 *
C                        ENDIF
 *
C                        ENDSR
```

FIGURE 9.2

ARYDIM2D Return Dimensional Indexes to 2D Array Template

```
... 1 ...+... 2 ...+... 3 ...+... 4 ...+... 5 ...+... 6 ...+... 7 ...+... 8
 *---------------------------------------------------------------------------
 * ARYDIM2D    Return dimensional indexes to 2D array template
 *
 * Function:
 *   Calculates the indexes to each of the individual dimensions
 *   to a two-dimensional array from the array index.
 *
 * Usage:
 *   Copy this template into your program and replace all
 *   &values listed below with your actual program variables.
 *   Syntax errors will occur if the array name is not
 *   three characters long.
 *
 * Expects:
 *   &ar    - array
 *   &dim1  - array_dim1_size
 *   &dim2  - array_dim2_size
 *   ARYIDX - array_index
 *
 * Returns:
 *   &idx1  - array_index1
 *   &idx2  - array_index2
 *   ARYERR - array_error on out of bounds index
 *---------------------------------------------------------------------------
```

continued

FIGURE 9.2 *CONTINUED*

```
... 1 ...+... 2 ...+... 3 ...+... 4 ...+... 5 ...+... 6 ...+... 7 ...+... 8
C           &arDIM    BEGSR
 *
C                     Z ADDARYIDX    ARYIDX  50
C                     MOVE *OFF      ARYERR   1
 *
C           @&arD1    IFEQ 0
C                     Z ADD&dim2     @&arD2  50
C           @&arD2    MULT &dim1     @&arD1  50
C                     ENDIF
 *
C           ARYIDX    IFLT 1
C           ARYIDX    ORGT @&arD1
 *
C                     MOVE *ON       ARYERR
C                     Z ADD0         &idx1
C                     Z ADD0         &idx2
C                     Z ADD0         &idx3
 *
C                     ELSE
 *
C           ARYIDX    DIV  @&arD2    @idx1
C                     MVR            @idx2
C           &idx2     IFEQ 0
C                     Z ADD@&arD2    @idx2
C                     ELSE
C                     ADD  1         &idx1
C                     ENDIF
 *
C                     ENDIF
 *
C                     ENDSR
```

In the following discussion, we focus on the templates for 3D arrays. All you need is a grasp of the basic concepts to use the templates for the 2D arrays, or to extend the principles to work with arrays of any dimension.

Let's see how to use the 3D array templates to implement a simple appointment-scheduling system. The system lets you schedule appointments for each hour of the working day, for each week of the year. To keep things simple, let's assume there are 10 working hours a day, 7 days a week, and 53 weeks per year. To code an array to store a description of each appointment requires 53 times 7 times 10 entries, or 3,710 total:

```
 *
 * Schedule array
E                    SCD        3710 30
 *
 * x,y,z dimensions of schedule
I              53                     C        SCDDWK
I               7                     C        SCDDDY
I              10                     C        SCDDHR
```

The SCD array holds the schedule, and the SCDD*xx* named constants define the week, day, and hour dimensions of the array.

You can access any x, y, or z coordinate in the array using the ARYIDX3D template (Figure 9.3).

FIGURE 9.3
ARYIDX3D Return Array Index to 3D Array Template

```
... 1 ...+... 2 ...+... 3 ...+... 4 ...+... 5 ...+... 6 ...+... 7 ...+... 8
 *-----------------------------------------------------------------------
 * ARYIDX3D   Return array index to 3D array template
 *
 * Function:
 *   Calculates the array index to a three-dimensional array
 *   from the indexes to each of the individual dimensions.
 *
 * Usage:
 *   Copy this template into your program and replace all
 *   &values listed below with your actual program variables.
 *   Syntax errors will occur if the array name is not
 *   three characters long.
 *
 * Expects:
 *   &ar   - array
 *   &dim1 - array_dim1_size
 *   &dim2 - array_dim2_size
 *   &dim3 - array_dim3_size
 *   &idx1 - array_index1
 *   &idx2 - array_index2
 *   &idx3 - array_index3
 *
 * Returns:
 *   ARYIDX - array_index
 *   ARYERR - array_error on out of bounds index
 *-----------------------------------------------------------------------
C           &arIDX    BEGSR
 *
C           @&arD1    IFEQ 0
C                     Z-ADD&dim3     @&arD3  50
C           @&arD3    MULT &dim2     @&arD2  50
C           @&arD2    MULT &dim1     @&arD1  50
C                     ENDIF
 *
C           &idx1     IFLT 1
C           &idx1     ORGT &dim1
C           &idx2     ORLT 1
C           &idx2     ORGT &dim2
C           &idx3     ORLT 1
C           &idx3     ORGT &dim3
 *
C                     Z-ADD0         ARYIDX  50
C                     MOVE *ON       ARYERR  1
 *
C                     ELSE
 *
C           &idx1     SUB  1         @&arI1  50
C                     MULT @&arD2    @&arI1
 *
C           &idx2     SUB  1         @&arI2  50
C                     MULT @&arD3    @&arI2
 *
C           &idx3     ADD  @&arI2    ARYIDX
C                     ADD  @&arI1    ARYIDX
C                     MOVE *OFF      ARYERR
```

continued

FIGURE **9.3** CONTINUED

```
... 1 ...+... 2 ...+... 3 ...+... 4 ...+... 5 ...+... 6 ...+... 7 ...+... 8
 *
C                     ENDIF
 *
C                     ENDSR
```

For example, to schedule an appointment with Clark Kent on the first hour of
day two of week 10, you first code

```
 *
 * Schedule appointment
C              'Clark'    CAT  'Kent':1  SCDNAM 30 P
C                         Z-ADD10        SCDIWK
C                         Z-ADD2         SCDIDY
C                         Z-ADD1         SCDIHR
C                         EXSR SCDIDX
C              ARYERR     IFEQ *OFF
C                         Z-ADDARYIDX    S        50
C                         MOVE SCDNAM    SCD,S
C                         ENDIF
```

The SCDIDX subroutine generated by the ARYIDX3D template translates the
week, day, and hour coordinates in the SCDI*xx* fields into the array index,
ARYIDX, which is used to load the appointment into the SCD array.

Next, you copy the ARYIDX3D template (Figure 9.3) into the source program at the end of the C-specs. Finally, you execute the following change
commands on the SEU command line to replace the generic values in the template with the specific values for the schedule array:

```
C   &ar      SCD     A
C   &dim1    SCDDWK  A
C   &dim2    SCDDDY  A
C   &dim3    SCDDHR  A
C   &idx1    SCDIWK  A
C   &idx2    SCDIDY  A
C   &idx3    SCDIHR  A
```

&ar is replaced by the array name SCD and creates a subroutine name of
SCDIDX. As in previous chapters, the array name must be three characters
long; otherwise, code can be shifted to the left or right, resulting in syntax
errors. &dim1 to &dim3 are replaced by the declared dimensions of the SCD
array, and &idx1 to &idx3 are replaced by the coordinates for the requried
array element.

Once the SCDIDX subroutine is in your program, you can access the SCD
array in other ways. For example, you could add the following code to process each appointment in the schedule in sequence:

```
 *
 * Process schedule
C              1         DO   SCDDWK   SCDIWK
C              1         DO   SCDDDY   SCDIDY
```

```
C               1              DO   SCDDHR    SCDIHR
C                              EXSR SCDIDX
C                              Z-ADDARYIDX    S
C                              MOVE SCD,S     SCDNAM
   *                          .process entry
C                              ENDDO
C                              ENDDO
C                              ENDDO
```

The nested DO loops set the coordinates for each hour of each day of each
week. Subroutine SCDIDX then translates the coordinates into array index
ARYIDX, so the appointment in the schedule can be processed.

You can also translate the RPG array index into the x, y, and z coordinates
for an array using the ARYDIM3D template (Figure 9.4).

FIGURE 9.4
ARYDIM3D Return Dimensional Indexes to 3D Array Template

```
... 1 ...+... 2 ...+... 3 ...+... 4 ...+... 5 ...+... 6 ...+... 7 ...+... 8
*------------------------------------------------------------------------
* ARYDIM3D - Return dimensional indexes to 3D array template
*
* Function:
*    Calculates the indexes to each of the individual dimensions
*    to a 3-dimensional array from the array index.
*
* Usage:
*    Copy this template into your program and replace all
*    &values listed below with your actual program variables.
*    Syntax errors will occur if the array name is not three
*    characters long.
*
* Expects:
*    &ar    - array
*    &dim1  - array_dim1_size
*    &dim2  - array_dim2_size
*    &dim3  - array_dim3_size
*    ARYIDX - array_index
*
* Returns:
*    &idx1  - array_index1
*    &idx2  - array_index2
*    &idx3  - array_index3
*    ARYERR - array_error on out of bounds index
*------------------------------------------------------------------------
C           &arDIM       BEGSR
   *
C                        Z-ADDARYIDX    ARYIDX 50
C                        MOVE *OFF       ARYERR 1
   *
C           a&arD1       IFEQ 0
C                        Z-ADD&dim3      a&arD3 50
C           a&arD3       MULT &dim2       a&arD2 50
C           a&arD2       MULT &dim1       a&arD1 50
C                        ENDIF
   *
C           ARYIDX       IFLT 1
C           ARYIDX       ORGT a&arD1
   *
```

continued

FIGURE 9.4 CONTINUED

```
... 1 ...+... 2 ...+... 3 ...+... 4 ...+... 5 ...+... 6 ...+... 7 ...+... 8
C                     MOVE *ON      ARYERR
C                     Z-ADD0        &idx1
C                     Z-ADD0        &idx2
C                     Z-ADD0        &idx3
 *
C                     ELSE
 *
C         ARYIDX      DIV  @&arD2   @idx1
C                     MVR           @idx2
C         &idx2       IFEQ 0
C                     Z-ADD@&arD2   @idx2
C                     ELSE
C                     ADD  1        &idx1
C                     ENDIF
 *
C         &idx2       DIV  @&arD3   @idx2
C                     MVR           @idx3
C         &idx3       IFEQ 0
C                     Z-ADD@&arD3   @idx3
C                     ELSE
C                     ADD  1        &idx2
C                     ENDIF
 *
C                     ENDIF
 *
C                     ENDSR
```

To find the first appointment in your schedule with Lois Lane, you first code

```
 *
 * Find appointment
C         'Lois'      CAT  'Lane':1 SCDNAM    P
C                     Z-ADD1        S
C         SCDNAM      LOKUP SCD,S                    99
 *
C         *IN99       IFEQ *ON
C                     Z-ADDS        ARYIDX
C                     EXSR SCDDIM
C         ARYERR      IFEQ *OFF
C                     .process appointment
C                     ENDIF
C                     ENDIF
```

The SCDDIM subroutine translates the array index ARYIDX into the SCDI*xx* coordinates for the week, day, and year. Just as with ARYIDX3D, you copy the ARYDIM3D template (Figure 9.4) into the source program at the end of the C-specs and perform the same SEU change commands to generate the finished version of the SCDDIM subroutine.

Chapter 10

Dynamically Determining Keypresses

Minimize indicator dependency and make your code more readable by using the AID byte to dynamically determine keypresses in interactive RPG programs, and to determine other keypresses beyond the function keys.

Like disk and printer files, display files also have a file information data structure. This data structure is defined in member WSDS, as shown in Figure 10.1.

FIGURE 10.1
WSDS RPG /COPY Member

```
... 1 ...+... 2 ...+... 3 ...+... 4 ...+... 5 ...+... 6 ...+... 7 ...+... 8
 *-----------------------------------------------------------------------
 * WSDS - Workstation display file info
 *
 * WSKEY   - Keypress value
 * WSCSR   - Binary cursor location
 * WSSFRN  - Current subfile relative record number
 * WSSRLR  - Current lowest subfile relative record number displayed
 * WSSFTR  - Total number of records in a subfile
 * WSWCSR  - Binary cursor location in a window
 *
 * Requires:
 *    WSDS data structure be named in display F-spec KINFDS
 *    continuation area of calling program.
 *-----------------------------------------------------------------------
IWSDS         DS
I                                        369 369 WSKEY
I                                      B 370 3710WSCSR
I                                      B 376 3770WSSFRN
I                                      B 378 3790WSSRLR
I                                      B 380 3810WSSFTR
I                                      B 382 3830WSWCSR
```

This abbreviated data structure contains all the relevant display-file-related values available in the file information data structure. For a detailed listing of what else is in this data structure, see the IBM *AS/400 RPG/400 Reference* (SC09-1817-00) and the IBM *AS/400 Data Management Guide* (SC41-3710-00).

Two of the most useful functions of the display file I/O feedback area are to determine the most recent key the operator pressed and to determine the current cursor position (discussed in Chapter 12).

RPG and DDS use indicators almost exclusively to communicate with each other. To minimize that indicator dependence between RPG and DDS, and to make your RPG easier to read, use the Attention Indicator (AID) byte to dynamically determine what key the operator presses in your RPG programs.

The AID byte is a 1-byte hexadecimal value reported back to your RPG program by way of the display file's I/O feedback area. By adding a data structure name in the display file's F-spec, and using two /COPY files, you can simply compare the AID byte to program constants to determine what key the operator pressed. Figure 10.2 shows WSCONS, the member that contains the named constants used to compare against the AID byte to determine the most recent keypress.

FIGURE 10.2
WSCONS RPG /COPY Member

```
... 1 ...+... 2 ...+... 3 ...+... 4 ...+... 5 ...+... 6 ...+... 7 ...+... 8
 *------------------------------------------------------------------
 * WSCONS - Named hexadecimal constants for function keys
 *------------------------------------------------------------------
I                    X'31'                 C         WSF01
I                    X'32'                 C         WSF02
I                    X'33'                 C         WSF03
I                    X'34'                 C         WSF04
I                    X'35'                 C         WSF05
I                    X'36'                 C         WSF06
I                    X'37'                 C         WSF07
I                    X'38'                 C         WSF08
I                    X'39'                 C         WSF09
I                    X'3A'                 C         WSF10
I                    X'3B'                 C         WSF11
I                    X'3C'                 C         WSF12
I                    X'B1'                 C         WSF13
I                    X'B2'                 C         WSF14
I                    X'B3'                 C         WSF15
I                    X'B4'                 C         WSF16
I                    X'B5'                 C         WSF17
I                    X'B6'                 C         WSF18
I                    X'B7'                 C         WSF19
I                    X'B8'                 C         WSF20
I                    X'B9'                 C         WSF21
I                    X'BA'                 C         WSF22
I                    X'BB'                 C         WSF23
I                    X'BC'                 C         WSF24
I                    X'BD'                 C         WSCLR
I                    X'F1'                 C         WSENTR
I                    X'F3'                 C         WSHELP
I                    X'F4'                 C         WSPGUP
I                    X'F5'                 C         WSPGDN
I                    X'F6'                 C         WSPRT
```

Figure 10.3 shows a snippet of a sample RPG program using these two members. Note that Figure 10.3 defines the name of the display file I/O feedback data structure as WSDS (because that is its name in the WSDS /COPY member) in the continuation line area of the F-spec. This continuation line definition of the file information data structure is required when using the /COPY members shown in this chapter.

FIGURE 10.3
Example RPG Snippet Using AID Byte and /COPY Members

```
... 1 ...+... 2 ...+... 3 ...+... 4 ...+... 5 ...+... 6 ...+... 7 ...+... 8
 * Note KINFDS continuation line naming WSDS data structure below
FWORKST  CF  E               WORKSTN     KINFDS WSDS
 *
 /COPY WSDS
 /COPY WSCONS
   :
C           SHOFMT    BEGSR
C                     EXFMTFMTNAME                  99
C                     SELEC
C           WSKEY     WHEQ WSF03
   :
   :                  F3 keypress action here
   :
C           WSKEY     WHEQ WSF05
   :
   :                  F3 keypress action here
   :
C           WSKEY     WHEQ WSENTR
   :
   :                  Enter keypress action here
   :
C                     ENDSL
C                     ENDSR
```

For even more readable code, you may want to extend this technique to actually map key assignments to more meaningful keypress names. For example, Figure 10.4 shows several of the most-used CUA key assignments mapped to named constants.

FIGURE 10.4
CUA Keypress Mnemonic Constants

```
... 1 ...+... 2 ...+... 3 ...+... 4 ...+... 5 ...+... 6 ...+... 7 ...+... 8
 *-----------------------------------------------------------------
 * WSCUA - Named CUA hex constants
 *-----------------------------------------------------------------
I           X'31'              C     HELP
I           X'33'              C     EXIT
I           X'34'              C     PROMPT
I           X'35'              C     REFRSH
I           X'36'              C     CREATE
I           X'37'              C     RETRV
I           X'3C'              C     CANCEL
I           X'B5'              C     TOP
I           X'B6'              C     BOTTOM
I           X'B7'              C     LEFT
I           X'B8'              C     RIGHT
I           X'BB'              C     OPTION
I           X'BC'              C     KEYS
```

Now, rather than checking for F3 or F5, your code can check for EXIT or REFRSH (Refresh) keystrokes. You can extend Figure 10.4 to include your shop's most common key assignments for user-defined keys. Be aware that, if you use Figure 10.4 as provided (unlike most of the members provided in this book), it does not use unique prefixes on its field names. We did this because we think a named constant of CANCEL makes infinitely more sense than WSCNCL — using contrived prefixes almost defeats the purpose of Figure 10.4's technique, given RPG's six-character field-name limits. If you use Figure 10.4 in your code, scour it carefully for field naming conflicts with your production code.

The next chapter shows how you can use the WSDS module for help with cursor positioning.

Chapter 11

Getting and Setting the Cursor Position

This technique dynamically gets and sets the cursor row and column position for your interactive programs.

The previous chapter showed how to use the display file information data structure to determine keypresses, but it can also be used to determine the current cursor position. The information data structure reports the cursor row and column position as a single binary value in positions 370–371. Dividing this value by 256 yields the current cursor row position, and the remainder of that division yields the current cursor column position. Using the WSDS RPG /COPY module from Chapter 10, the following RPG snippet shows how to determine the cursor position:

```
FWORKST   CF  E                    WORKSTN      KINFDS WSDS
 *
I/COPY WSDS
 *
   :
 *
C                      EXFMTFMTNAME              99
C* Determine cursor row and column position
C         WSCSR    DIV  256         #CSROW  20
C                  MVR              #CSCOL  30
```

Note that a 3-digit integer is used to hold the column position in case a 132-column workstation is being used. Remember also that using the WSDS /COPY member requires that the display file F-spec specify a KINFDS continuation line to name the WSDS data structure for the display file being used.

In addition to determining the cursor position on the screen, the file information data structure can also be used to determine the cursor position in an active window. The same technique shown here applies, but for windows you must use the WSWCSR field (in position 383 and in position 383 of the file information data structure). The coordinates reported by this field are always relative to the upper left corner of the window.

If you need to know more than just the cursor position, the DDS keyword RTNCSRLOC returns not only the cursor position, but also the name of the display format and the field on which the cursor is located. It can even tell you the cursor's position in the field. You specify the RTNCSRLOC keyword in the format shown in Figure 11.1.

FIGURE 11.1
DDS to Set the Cursor Location

```
... 1 ...+... 2 ...+... 3 ...+... 4 ...+... 5 ...+... 6 ...+... 7 ...+... 8
A           RFMT01
A                                           RTNCSRLOC(&CSRRCD +
A                                                    &CSRFLD +
A                                                    &CSRPOS)
A  05                                       CSRLOC(ROW COL)
A           CSRRCD        10A   H
A           CSRFLD        10A   H
A           CSRPOS         4S  0H
A           ROW            3S  0H
A           COL            3S  0H
A           OPTION         1A   B   1   2
A           CUSNBR         7S  0B   1   5
```

You must always specify RTNCSRLOC with two or three variables that refer to hidden fields in the display file, as the figure shows. OS/400's display management routines place the cursor position feedback information into these fields. Field CSRRCD will contain the name of the record format within which the cursor is located, and field CSRFLD will contain the name of the field. If the cursor is not located in a valid record or field, the respective field will be blank.

The third return variable used with RTNCSRLOC (&CSRPOS) is optional. If your application needs to know where the cursor is located within a field on the screen, you can use this keyword to return that information. As a result of the coding in Figure 11.1, for example, if the user presses Enter while the cursor is in the third position of the CUSNBR field, the RTNCSRLOC feature will return CSRRCD with the value FMT01, CSRFLD with the value CUSNBR, and CSRPOS with the value 3.

Be sure to define each of these fields (CSRRCD, CSRFLD, and CSRPOS) with the same data types and lengths as the examples shown. Also, note that you precede each variable with an ampersand (&) when you specify it as an argument in the RTNCSRLOC keyword, similar to the way you specify variables in a CL program.

Besides finding out where your cursor came from, you can tell it where to go. The DDS cursor-positioning function, DSPATR(PC), has been around since the early days, of course. But you may not know about the more recent CSRLOC (cursor location) DDS keyword, which lets you specify the coordinates where you want the cursor to appear when your program displays the screen. In Figure 11.1, CSRLOC specifies two fields, ROW and COL, which refer to hidden 3-byte, zoned-decimal fields in the display file. You put into these fields the values of the row and the column where you want the cursor to be when your program displays the screen. Notice that you can set an option indicator (e.g., indicator 05 in the figure) if you want to condition the cursor location, but you can only specify it once for each record format. If

CSRLOC and DSPATR(PC) are in effect for a single output operation to a display, CSRLOC takes precedence over DSPATR(PC).

For applications that use subfiles, there are analogous cursor manipulation functions that apply especially to subfiles. The SFLCSRRRN keyword (available in V2R2 and greater) returns to your program the relative record number of the subfile record in which your cursor is positioned. SFLRCDNBR(CURSOR) lets you specify cursor positioning on a specific subfile record.

Chapter 12

Using Named Indicators with Interactive Programs

Use this indicator "swindle" to make your interactive RPG programs more readable and easier to maintain.

RPG almost goes out of its way to make itself hard to read. Its painfully short field names and rigid columns are trouble enough, but its dogged reliance on indicators to communicate with DDS panels is especially frustrating. Here is a technique you can use to map meaningful (meaningful within RPG/400's 6-character definition of meaningful!) names to screen-attribute and user-input indicators.

This technique relies on two include members, INDDS and INGETPUT. INDDS (Figure 12.1) defines a 99-byte data structure used to map *IN indicator values.

FIGURE 12.1
INDDS Indicator /COPY Module

```
... 1 ...+... 2 ...+... 3 ...+... 4 ...+... 5 ...+... 6 ...+... 7 ...+... 8
 *----------------------------------------------------------------------
 * INDDS  -  Array of user indicators (corresponds to *IN).
 *
 * Function:
 *   Used with GETIND and PUTIND (in member INGETPUT) to get and
 *   put values in *IN indicator array.
 *----------------------------------------------------------------------
 *
IINDDS       DS
I I              '00000000000000000000-   1  99 #IND
I                '00000000000000000000-
I                '00000000000000000000-
I                '00000000000000000000-
I                '00000000000000000000'
```

INGETPUT (Figure 12.2) provides two short subroutines to tranfer indicator values between INDDS's data structure and RPG's *IN indicator array.

FIGURE 12.2
INGETPUT Indicator Get and Put /COPY Module

```
... 1 ...+... 2 ...+... 3 ...+... 4 ...+... 5 ...+... 6 ...+... 7 ...+... 8
 *-----------------------------------------------------------------------
 * INGETPUT  -  Get or put indicator array.
 *
 * Function:
 *   These two subroutines get and put indicator values in *IN.
 *   It is usually used for screen attribute control or to
 *   manage user input with interactive programs.
 *
 *-----------------------------------------------------------------------
 * INDGET - Get indicator values from *IN
 *-----------------------------------------------------------------------
C           INDGET      BEGSR
 *
C                       MOVEA*IN        INDDS
 *
C                       ENDSR
 *
 *-----------------------------------------------------------------------
 * INDPUT - Put indicator values into *IN
 *-----------------------------------------------------------------------
C           INDPUT      BEGSR
 *
C                       MOVEAINDDS      *IN
 *
C                       ENDSR
```

To use this technique, include the INDDS member somewhere in your
RPG program's I-specs and the INGETPUT member somewhere in the subroutine section of your C-specs. To "map" indicator positions to field names, add
additional I-specs immediately under the INDDS /COPY statement. In the
example below, nine data structure subfields provide field names for subfile
events, keystroke events, and screen attributes that can occur in the program.

```
  /COPY INDDS
I                                              33  33 #SFTOP
I                                              34  34 #SFBOT
I                                              60  60 #PROT
I                                              80  80 #SFLCR
I                                              81  81 #SFDSP
I                                              82  82 #SFEND
I                                              90  90 #POSTO
I                                              91  91 #PGUP
I                                              92  92 #PGDN
```

For example, #PROT is mapped to indicator 60, which is used in the DDS
to protect some input fields when a given circumstance occurs. By using this
technique, you simply set the value of #PROT without needing to worry about
what actual indicator value is being referenced.

After including these members, all you need to do to put them to work is,
immediately before any workstation output, call the INDPUT subroutine to
transfer indicator values from INDDS's indicator structure to the *IN array; and

immediately after any workstation output, call the INDGET subroutine to transfer *IN indicator values into INDDS's indicator structure.

Notice in the code below that *ON is used to set the #PROT mapped indicator on. To set values in the INDDS data structure, you can use RPG's *ON and *OFF figurative constants. These constants simply move a 1 or a 0 into a character-based field; and they can be used with any character-based field, not just RPG indicators.

```
 /COPY INDDS
I                                         33  33 #SFTOP
I                                         34  34 #SFBOT
I                                         60  60 #PROT
I                                         80  80 #SFLCR
I                                         81  81 #SFDSP
I                                         82  82 #SFEND
I                                         90  90 #POSTO
I                                         91  91 #PGUP
I                                         92  92 #PGDN
 :

 *------------------------------------------------------------
 * DSPLST - Display list
 *------------------------------------------------------------
C           DSPLST    BEGSR
 *
 * Manually set any mapped indicators as needed here.
 * In this example, an indicator used to control the
 * protect-input attribute of some fields is enabled,
 * if the condition calls for it.
 *
C           COND      IFEQ PROTEC
C                     MOVE *ON        #PROT
C                     ELSE
C                     MOVE *OFF       #PROT
C                     ENDIF
 *
C                     EXSR INDPUT
C                     EXFMTSFLCTL
C                     EXSR INDGET
 :
C           *INKE     CASEQ*ON        RFSLST
C           *INKF     CASEQ*ON        PRCOPT
C           *INKL     CASEQ*ON        CNLPGM
C           #POSTO    CASEQ*ON        INZLST
C           #PGDN     CASEQ*ON        PAGEDN
C           #PGUP     CASEQ*ON        PAGEUP
C                     ENDCS
 :
 *
 * Subsequent routines could check the values of other
 * mapped values to test for specific actions. For example,
 * #SFTOP and #SFBOT could be checked to see if the subfile
 * is positioned at the top or the bottom of the subfile.
 *
 :
C                     ENDSR
 :
 /COPY INGETPUT
 :
```

Chapter 13

Using a Message Subfile to Display Error Messages

Enhance your programs' messaging capabilities by harnessing the power of message subfiles and the program message queue.

Taking advantage of OS/400's superb messaging facilities to display program messages adds a level of professionalism to your applications and makes it easy to externalize (and therefore reuse) program messages. Because second-level help is built into this messaging system, messages displayed this way easily provide an increased level of information to your users. Also, depending on your design criteria, using the program message queue makes it possible to send more than one error message at a time to a program message queue. As illustrated with the code provided in this chapter, though, you can limit the number of error messages the operator sees at once (we recommend displaying messages one at a time).

This chapter shows how to harness the power of program message queues to provide this messaging facility for your application programs. Figure 13.1 shows an example screen displaying one message from the program message queue.

FIGURE 13.1
Message Displayed from the Program Message Queue

```
    Input field.................         █_____

    F3=Exit   F13=Send messages   F14=Clear messages
    This is the first message using variable data: Hi there
```

The plus sign near the right edge of the screen indicates there are other messages for the operator to see (these additional messages can be seen using the
Page Up and Page Down keys). To display second-level Help, all the operator
needs to do is put the cursor anywhere on the message and press the Help
key; any available second-level Help will then be displayed.

The program, MSGERR, which displays the screen shown in Figure 13.1, is
shown in Figure 13.2; the display file DDS, MSGERRD, is shown in Figure 13.3.

FIGURE 13.2

Example Program Using an Error Message Subfile

```
... 1 ...+... 2 ...+... 3 ...+... 4 ...+... 5 ...+... 6 ...+... 7 ...+... 8
 /COPY CTLWDMP
 *
FMSGERRD CF  E                      WORKSTN     KINFDS WSDS
 *
 /COPY ERRDS
 /COPY MSGDS
 /COPY PGMSDS
 /COPY STDTYPES
 /COPY WSCONS
 /COPY WSCUA
 /COPY WSDS
 *
C                      MOVEL*OFF      EXTPGM
 *
C          EXTPGM      DOWNE*ON
 *
 * Write error message subfile
C                      WRITEMSGCTL
 *
 * Write and read workstation format:
C                      EXFMTSCREEN
 *
C                      SELEC
 * Stop when EXIT key is pressed
C          WSKEY       WHEQ EXIT
C                      MOVEL*ON       EXTPGM
 *
 * Send three messages to program queue
C          WSKEY       WHEQ WSF13
C                      EXSR SNDM
 *
 * Clear all messages from program queue
C          WSKEY       WHEQ WSF14
C                      EXSR MSGCLR
 *
C                      ENDSL
 *
C                      ENDDO
 *
C                      MOVEL*ON       *INLR
 *
C                      RETRN
 *
 *
C          *INZSR      BEGSR
 *
C          *LIKE       DEFN #BOOL      EXTPGM
```

continued

FIGURE **13.2** CONTINUED

```
... 1 ...+... 2 ...+... 3 ...+... 4 ...+... 5 ...+... 6 ...+... 7 ...+... 8
 *
C                   ENDSR
 *
 *
C           SNDM      BEGSR
 *
 * Set message file and library
C                     MOVEL'USRERRS' MSGF      P
C                     MOVEL'*LIBL'   MSGL      p
 * Set message type
C                     MOVELMSDIAG    MSGTYP    P
 * Set message queue and stack
C                     MOVELMSCURQ    MSGQ      P
C                     Z-ADDMSCSTK    MSGSTK
 *
 * Send USR0001 with program name as variable data:
C                     MOVEL'USR0001' MSGID     P
C                     MOVEL'Hi there'MSGTXT    P
C                     Z-ADD8         MSGLEN
C                     EXSR MSGSND
 *
 * Send USR0002 (no variable data):
C                     MOVEL'USR0002' MSGID
C                     EXSR MSGSND
 *
 * Send USR0003 (no variable data):
C                     MOVEL'USR0003' MSGID
C                     EXSR MSGSND
 *
C                   ENDSR
 *
 /COPY MSGSND
 /COPY MSGCLR
 /COPY PSSR
```

FIGURE **13.3**
Example DDS to Implement an Error Message Subfile

```
... 1 ...+... 2 ...+... 3 ...+... 4 ...+... 5 ...+... 6 ...+... 7 ...+... 8
A                                   DSPSIZ( 24 80 *DS3 )
A                                   PRINT
 *-----------------------------------------------------------------------
 * Input record
 *-----------------------------------------------------------------------
A           R SCREEN
A                                   CF03 CF13 CF14
A                                   OVERLAY
 *
A                                     4  8'Input field...................'
A           WKNAME      24   B  4 40
A                                    23  2'F3=Exit'
A                                    23 11'F13=Send messages'
A                                    23 30'F14=Clear messages'
 *-----------------------------------------------------------------------
 * Error message subfile
 *-----------------------------------------------------------------------
```

continued

FIGURE 13.3 *CONTINUED*

```
... 1 ...+... 2 ...+... 3 ...+... 4 ...+... 5 ...+... 6 ...+... 7 ...+... 8
A           R MSGSFL                         SFL
A                                            SFLMSGRCD(24)
A             MSGKEY                         SFLMSGKEY
A             PSPGM                          SFLPGMQ
 *
 *---------------------------------------------------------------------
 * Error message subfile control record
 *---------------------------------------------------------------------
A           R MSGCTL                         SFLCTL(MSGSFL)
A                                            OVERLAY
A N99                                        SFLDSP SFLDSPCTL SFLINZ SFLEND
A                                            SFLSIZ(2) SFLPAG(1)
A             PSPGM                          SFLPGMQ
```

MSGERR makes substantial use of previously referenced /COPY members, and this chapter adds three new ones: MSGDS, an RPG I-spec /COPY member (Figure 13.4) that provides several messaging-related variables and constants; and MSGSND and MSGCLR, RPG C-spec /COPY members (Figure 13.5 and Figure 13.6) that provide subroutines to send and clear program messages from a program message queue (these subroutines call two OS/400 message-related APIs). To use these two members, include MSGDS somewhere in your program's I-specs and include MSGSND and MSGCLR somewhere in the subroutine section of your program's C-specs.

FIGURE 13.4

Member MSGDS

```
... 1 ...+... 2 ...+... 3 ...+... 4 ...+... 5 ...+... 6 ...+... 7 ...+... 8
 *---------------------------------------------------------------------
 * MSGDS - Declares messaging-related variables and constants
 *
 * Function:
 *   Defines the MSGDTA data structure which declares several
 *   messaging-related variables and several messaging-related
 *   constants.
 *
 * MSGDTA - Messaging-related data structure variables:
 *    MSGID    - Message ID
 *    MSGF     - Message file
 *    MSGL     - Message library
 *      MSGFL     - Message file and library
 *    MSGTXT   - Message variable text
 *    MSGLEN   - Length of variable text
 *    MSGTYP   - Message type
 *    MSGQ     - Message queue
 *    MSGSTK   - Message stack
 *    MSGKEY   - Message key
 *    MSGNTY   - Message number type
 *    MSGPQ    - Message program queue
 *    MSGRMV   - Messages to remove
 *    MSGCNT   - Message count
 *
```

continued

FIGURE 13.4 *CONTINUED*

```
... 1 ...+... 2 ...+... 3 ...+... 4 ...+... 5 ...+... 6 ...+... 7 ...+... 8
 * Messaging-related constants:
 *    MSBLK   - Blank
 *    MSNUL   - Null
 *    MSALL   - *ALL
 *    MSDIAG  - *DIAG
 *    MSESC   - *ESCAPE
 *    MSCSTK  - Current program stack  (0)
 *    MSPSTK  - Previous program stack (1)
 *    MSCURQ  - Current program queue  (*)
 *    MSLAST  - Last message sentinel text
 *    MSMAXM  - Maximum occurrences in ERRTBL data structure
 *-----------------------------------------------------------------------
IMSDDTA      IDS
I I              ' '                   1    7 MSGID
I I              ' '                   8   17 MSGF
I I              ' '                  18   27 MSGL
I                                      8   27 MSGFL
I I              ' '                  28  106 MSGTXT
I I              79              B  107 1100MSGLEN
I I              ' '                 111  120 MSGTYP
I I              '*'                 121  130 MSGQ
I I              0               B  131 1340MSGSTK
I I              ' '                 135  138 MSGKEY
I I              1               B  157 1600MSGNTY
I I              '*'                 161  170 MSGPQ
I I              ' '                 171  180 MSGRMV
I I              0                   181 1900MSGCNT
 *
I                ' '            C              MSBLK
I                0              C              MSNUL
I                '*ALL'         C              MSALL
I                '*DIAG'        C              MSDIAG
I                '*ESCAPE'      C              MSESC
I                0              C              MSCSTK
I                1              C              MSPSTK
I                '*'            C              MSCURQ
I                '*LAST'        C              MSLAST
I                99             C              MSMAXM
```

FIGURE 13.5

Member MSGSND

```
... 1 ...+... 2 ...+... 3 ...+... 4 ...+... 5 ...+... 6 ...+... 7 ...+... 8
 *-----------------------------------------------------------------------
 * MSGSND - Send a message to a program message queue.
 *
 * Function:
 *    Send the message from a message file to a program message queue.
 *
 * Requires copy modules:
 *    ERRDS   - Error data structure
 *    MSGDS   - Messaging-related data structure
 *
 * Expects:
 *    MSGID   - Message ID
 *    MSGF    - Message file
 *    MSGL    - Message library
 *    MSGTXT  - Message replacement text (optional)
 *    MSGLEN  - Length of message replacement text (optional)
```

continued

FIGURE 13.5 *CONTINUED*

```
... 1 ...+... 2 ...+... 3 ...+... 4 ...+... 5 ...+... 6 ...+... 7 ...+... 8
*    MSGTYP   - Message type
*    MSGQ     - Call message queue
*    MSGSTK   - Call stack counter
*    MSGKEY   - Message key (always blanks)
*    ERRDS    - Error data structure
*
* Returns:
*    ERRDS    - Standard API error data structure
*
*------------------------------------------------------------------------
C           MSGSND    BEGSR
 *
C                     CALL 'QMHSNDPM'
C                     PARM           MSGID
C                     PARM           MSGFL
C                     PARM           MSGTXT
C                     PARM           MSGLEN
C                     PARM           MSGTYP
C                     PARM           MSGQ
C                     PARM           MSGSTK
C                     PARM           MSGKEY
C                     PARM           ERRDS
 *
C                     ENDSR
```

FIGURE 13.6

Member MSGCLR

```
... 1 ...+... 2 ...+... 3 ...+... 4 ...+... 5 ...+... 6 ...+... 7 ...+... 8
*------------------------------------------------------------------------
* MSGCLR - Remove all messages from program message queue.
*
* Function:
*   Extracts all messages from the current program's message queue.
*
* Requires copy modules:
*    ERRDS    - Error data structure
*    MSGDS    - Messaging-related data structure
*
* Expects:
*    MSCURQ   - Messages from current queue
*    MSCSTK   - Messages from current program
*    MSALL    - Remove all messages
*    ERRDS    - Error data structure
*
* Returns:
*    ERRDS    - Standard API error data structure
*
*------------------------------------------------------------------------
C           MSGCLR    BEGSR
 *
C                     MOVELMSCURQ    MSGQ      P
C                     MOVELMSCSTK    MSGSTK    P
C                     MOVE *BLANKS   MSGKEY
C                     MOVELMSALL     MSGRMV    P
 *
C                     CALL 'QMHRMVPM'
```

continued

FIGURE **13.6** *CONTINUED*

```
... 1 ...+... 2 ...+... 3 ...+... 4 ...+... 5 ...+... 6 ...+... 7 ...+... 8
C                    PARM            MSGQ
C                    PARM            MSGSTK
C                    PARM            MSGKEY
C                    PARM            MSGRMV
C                    PARM            ERRDS
 *
C                    ENDSR
```

You'll also need to include two message subfile-related record formats in your program's display file DDS. These two record formats are shown in the shaded area in Figure 13.3 and should be copied "as is" to your display file DDS — there is nothing application-specific in them. Although indicator 99 is referenced with the SFLEND keyword, the code works regardless of the status of indicator 99 (the SLFEND keyword requires an option indicator, but as coded here doesn't use it). The DDS keyword SFLPGMQ (subfile program message queue) links the subfile coded in these DDS specs to the program message queue of the program specified in the variable PSPGM (which is obtained from the program information data structure, defined in /COPY member PGMSDS — see Chapter 2).

In your RPG program, just before a display file write operation (either with the WRITE or EXFMT opcodes), write the MSGCTL display file subfile record (shown being written in the shaded lines in Figure 13.2). If no messages are in the program message queue, none are displayed; otherwise, messages in the queue will be displayed one at a time, and you can use the Page up and Page down keys to display others. When messages are displayed in this way, the keyboard isn't locked and the cursor remains at its current input field position. Note that it is very important that any display file formats displayed after the error message subfile has been displayed have the record-level DDS keyword OVERLAY associated with them; if they don't, the message subfile area will be cleared before the operator sees it.

In program MSGERR, the SNDM subroutine (called when F13 is pressed) sends three messages to the program message queue. Generally, you will condition sending messages on some kind of input-verifying code; in this example, MSGERR unconditionally sends three messages to simply illustrate the concept. To send a message, you need to provide the following parameters:

MSGF	Name of the message file from which messages should be displayed.
MSGL	Name of the message file library.
MSGTYP	Message type. You'll almost always send *DIAG messages, which is indicated with the MSDIAG constant.
MSGQ	Program message queue. You can send messages to the current program queue or to the external message queue. In this case, you'll want to send them to the current program queue, which is indicated with the MSCURQ constant.

MSGST Program call stack. This is a numeric value that indicates how many programs up the invocation stack messages should be sent. For example, to send them to program A from program A, use a MSGSTK value of 0 (which is indicated with the constant value of MSCSTK). If program A called program B, and you wanted program B to send messages to program A's queue, you would use a call stack value of 1 (as indicated by the constant MSPSTK). Only values 0 and 1 have constants provided for them, but you may need to code other level values depending on how nested your programs get.

MSGID Message ID. This is the 7-character message ID of the OS/400 message to display.

MSGTXT Variable message text. If the message uses variable text, this variable lets you provide up to 79 characters of variable message text.

MSGLEN Length of variable message text. This variable must define the length of the variable message text provided. For messages that don't provide variable text, set MSGTXT to blanks and MSGLEN to zero.

Examine subroutine SNDM closely in Figure 13.2 to see how these variables are being displayed to send program messages.

To remove messages from its program message queue, MSGERR simply calls subroutine MSGCLR (shown in the /COPY member MSGCLR in Figure 13.6) when F14 is pressed. This routine is intended to be called from the program from which you want to remove messages; thus, you don't have to specify the program message queue or program call stack for this routine. While the example program unconditionally removes the messages on a simple keystroke, your application logic will generally remove them after field validation and after the operator has seen the messages and corrected the errors indicated.

The only other thing you need to do to display program messages is to have messages to display. For that, you can use the WRKMSGD command to interactively maintain a message file. Alternatively, you can use the ADDMSGD command (as shown below) to add messages one at a time to a message file.

```
ADDMSGD MSGID( USR0001 )                                        +
        MSGF( *LIBL/USRERRS )                                   +
        MSG( 'This is the first message using variable data: &1' ) +
        SECLVL( 'This is the first message second level help' )  +
        FMT( ( *CHAR 8 ) )
```

One last general note about program MSGERR (Figure 13.2): Note how this program illustrates the concept of building programs quickly from proven, tested chunks of reusable code. MSGERR is only 78 lines long; yet when all the /COPY members are included (automatically, by the RPG compiler), MSGERR expands to more than 400 lines of code. As you can see, MSGERR was easier to write, and easier to test, using the /COPY modules, than it would have been to write all 400+ lines from scratch. In this case, less than 20 percent of the RPG required to write a complete program had to be written from scratch.

Chapter 14

Using Data Structures
as Program Parameters

**Power-up the capability of called programs to "talk" to each other by
using data structures as program parameters.**

Using called RPG programs is an effective way to write modular, robust applications that are easy to maintain. At first glance, though, the capability appears a bit constrained because the types of parameters you can pass from program to program seem limited to simple program variables. This chapter debunks that myth and shows you how to add to RPG's program-call capabilities by using data structures as program parameters. Like several of the programs in this book, the programs presented in this chapter use some routines from previous chapters. Before we discuss using data structures as parameters, let's review RPG's method of passing parameters from one program to another.

In RPG, parameters are passed by reference — that is, the address of a parameter, not a parameter's actual value, is what is actually passed from program to program. Consider the following snippets:

```
 * Program A
C                       Z-ADD5        TSTVAL 150
C                       CALL PGMB                     99
C                       PARM          TSTVAL
 * TSTVAL now equal to 15 in Program A

 * Program B
C           *ENTRY    PLIST
C                     PARM TSTVAL
C                     ADD  10       TSTVAL
C                     RETRN
```

Before calling Program B, Program A sets the value of TSTVAL to 5. After the call to Program B, though, the value of TSTVAL in Program A is 15 — because Program B added 10 to TSTVAL. This change in the value of TSTVAL is reflected in Program A because the address of TSTVAL was passed to Program B — thus, any changes Program B made to the value stored at that address would be reflected in Program A (or any other program to which TSTVAL had been passed). It's important to realize that Program A didn't pass the value of field TSTVAL to Program B; Program A simply passed the address of field TSTVAL to Program B.

This concept of passing addresses rather than actual values is behind RPG's ability to pass multiple-occurrence data structures (MODS) from program to program — the actual data structure isn't passed, merely the *address* of the data structure. Using a multiple-occurrence data structure is an excellent way to pass a variable number of parameters between programs. We use them extensively with interactive work-with programs to pass lists of selected records (and associated data) to subprograms, but the technique has many other uses.

While it's not absolutely necessary, the first step we recommend you take when using multiple-occurrence data structures for program parameters is to create a /COPY member that describes the data structure you'll be using as a parameter. With a /COPY member, you can be sure the multiple-occurrence data structure will be defined correctly and consistently in every program that references it. Figure 14.1 shows an example /COPY member.

FIGURE 14.1
/COPY Member with Multiple-Occurrence Data Structure Definition

```
... 1 ...+... 2 ...+... 3 ...+... 4 ...+... 5 ...+... 6 ...+... 7 ...+... 8
 *
ICUSINF      DS                            99
I                                           1   7ØCUSNO
I                                           8  37 CUSNAM
I                                          38  52 CUSPH1
I                                          53  67 CUSPH2
I                                          67  772CUSBAL
 *
I             99                      C          CUMAX
 *
I            IDS
I                                           1  15ØCUENTS
```

In this example, a 99-occurrence data structure is defined that will be used to pass customer information for up to 99 customers from one program to another. Each occurrence includes the customer's number, name, two telephone numbers, and the customer's account balance. The maximum number of occurrences you require will depend on your application. In this case, we assume that users typically won't attempt to select more than 99 customers to work with at once.

The member in Figure 14.1 also defines a constant and a field that programs need to reference this structure. The named constant CUMAX defines the maximum occurrence that can be stored in, or otherwise referenced in, the CUSINF data structure (this number cannot be determined dynamically in RPG). If you change the number of occurrences (in positions 44–47 of the first line of the data structure declaration) of the CUSINF data structure, you must also change the constant value of CUMAX accordingly (also, don't forget to recompile all programs that use the data structure's /COPY member). The field declared in this member, CUENTS, will be used to track the actual number of occurrences being referenced in the CUSINF data structure. By declaring the data structure, the named constant, and the one field in one

/COPY member, you ensure that all RPG programs will automatically have access to the data they need to work with the CUSINF data structure.

Figure 14.2 shows the stub of an RPG program filling 24 occurrences of CUSINF and then passing that data structure to another RPG program.

FIGURE 14.2

Passing a Multiple-Occurrence Data Structure to a Program

```
... 1 ...+... 2 ...+... 3 ...+... 4 ...+... 5 ...+... 6 ...+... 7 ...+... 8
 /COPY CUSINF
  :
  :
 * Fill 24 DS entries with data
 C           1          DO   24        X
 C           X          OCUR CUSINF
 C                      .. fill CUSINF structure here
 C                      ENDDO
 C                      Z-ADD24         CUENTS
  *
 C                      CALL 'PGMA'
 C                      PARM            CUSINF
 C                      PARM            CUENTS
```

The CUSINF data structure can contain up to 99 occurrences and the CUENTS field is used to signal to the called program how many of them actually contain active data. Note that the CUSINF data structure and the CUENTS field are both passed to the called program. The called program will use CUENTS to determine how many of the 99 occurrences of CUSINF it should process.

Figure 14.3 shows a stub of the program called from the stub shown in Figure 14.2.

FIGURE 14.3

Processing the Passed Data Structure

```
... 1 ...+... 2 ...+... 3 ...+... 4 ...+... 5 ...+... 6 ...+... 7 ...+... 8
 /COPY CUSINF
 C           *ENTRY     PLIST
 C                      PARM            CUSINF
 C                      PARM            CUENTS
  :
 * Check for maximum entries exceeded.
 C           CUENTS     IFGT CUMAX
  : Error processing here for maximum entries exceeded
 C                      ENDIF
  *
 * Read each occurrence of the CUSINF passed.
 C           1          DO   CUENTS    X
 C           X          OCUR CUSINF
  :                     .. do something with an
  :                     .. occurrence of CUSINF here
 C                      ENDDO
```

To ensure that the calling program doesn't misinform the called program, this stub provides a defensive test to ensure that the number of CUSINF entries to process doesn't exceed what the called program thinks is the maximum number of occurrences for CUSINF (based on the value of CUMAX). This test ensures that the calling program didn't put an inappropriate value in the CUENTS field. After ensuring that CUENTS is okay, the called program then reads the specified number of occurrences from the CUSINF data structure. In this example, each occurrence can be put in a subfile so a user can display data and further work with the customer data received.

The technique presented in this chapter shows how to pass a specific multiple-occurrence data structure as a program parameter. While the examples are all specialized to work with the CUSINF data structure, you can easily create your own data structures to use as parameters. The technique of passing a multiple-occurrence data structure as a parameter has many interesting and useful purposes. You'll find that giving just a little thought to creating reusable routines to manage the process easily produces good results.

If you are skeptical of this technique because of performance implications, relax. Because an address is being passed rather than actual data, using a multiple-occurrence data structure — of any size — as a program parameter has no more performance impact than passing the address of a single integer value. Further, the technique is actually a memory-saving technique, because the actual data structure only exists in one program; other programs are simply acessing the already-existing data structure in that program.

Chapter 15

Ending Interactive Programs Automatically

Avoid potential security problems and annoying operational interruptions by ending unattended interactive programs automatically and gracefully.

You can have level 40 security active on your AS/400, change passwords frequently, and be diligent about managing object authorization; but even the simplest thing can render all this defensive security planning useless. For example, consider the payroll manager who walks away from a sensitive payroll application for what was to be just a few minutes — but ends up recounting a recent skiing trip in excruciating detail near the company coffee pot for 45 minutes. While the manager is telling her skiing story, the sensitive application she was using, not to mention her signed-on interactive session, are at the mercy of any prying eyes or fingertips that make their way to her empty desk.

Beyond security concerns, consider the interactive application that is accidentally left open overnight, keeping nighttime processing from acquiring exclusive use of database files for maintenance or purging. It's very annoying to arrive early in the morning to discover that nighttime processing didn't end normally because an active application interfered.

With just a little extra coding, you can avoid either of these scenarios by adding the logic to your RPG programs to cause them to end in a planned, graceful fashion. You can implement this technique with a little "swindle" using the DDS INVITE keyword, which is normally intended for use with multiple acquired devices attached to a display file. In this case, we're only using one device per program. The CRTDSPF's WAITRCD parameter, which specifies a time-out value, can be used to create a display file that will trigger a time-out event to which your RPG program can react.

To see the technique in action, use the following command to compile the DDS shown in Figure 15.1:

```
CRTDSPF FILE( library/dspf )        +
        SRCFILE( library/srcfile )  +
        WAITRCD( 15 )
```

FIGURE 15.1
DDS to Achieve Screen Time-Out

```
... 1 ...+... 2 ...+... 3 ...+... 4 ...+... 5 ...+... 6 ...+... 7 ...+... 8
 * DDS to achieve screen time-out.
 *
 * Use the following CRTDSPF command to create this display file.
 *
 * The WAITRCD parameter specifies, in seconds, the time the display
 * waits for input.
 *
 *    CRTDSPF FILE( library/dspf )          +
 *            SRCFILE( library/srcfile )    +
 *            WAITRCD( 15 )
 *
 *
 A                                      DSPSIZ( 24 80 *DS3 )
 A                                      PRINT
 A                                      INVITE
 *-------------------------------------------------------------------
 * Input format SCREEN1
 *-------------------------------------------------------------------
 A           R SCREEN1
 A                                      CF03 CF12
 *
 A                                      1 36'Screen #1'
 A                                      4  8'Screen #1 input field.........'
 A             WKNAME        24    B  4 40
 A                                     15  2'Program automatically ends-
 A                                           after 15 seconds of-
 A                                           inactivity.'
 A                                     23  2'F3=Exit'
 A                                     23 11'F12=CANCEL'
 *-------------------------------------------------------------------
 * Input format SCREEN2
 *-------------------------------------------------------------------
 A           R SCREEN2
 A                                      CF03 CF12
 *
 A                                      1 36'Screen #2'
 A                                      4  8'Screen #2 input field.........'
 A             WKNAME        24    B  4 40
 A                                     15  2'Panel automatically ends-
 A                                           after 15 seconds of-
 A                                           inactivity.'
 A                                     23  2'F3=Exit'
 A                                     23 11'F12=CANCEL'
```

The WAITRCD value specifies how long any one screen format in the resulting display file will be displayed before a time-out occurs. Within the DDS specifications, note the use of the file-level keyword INVITE. WAITRCD is only valid for read-from-invited-devices operations; thus, the INVITE keyword is necessary. Providing a WAITRCD value with the CRTDSPF command and having a file-level keyword are the only two display file special conditions for this technique.

The corresponding RPG program for the DDS in Figure 15.1 is shown in Figure 15.2.

Figure 15.2

RPG Program Illustrating Screen Time-Out

```
... 1 ...+... 2 ...+... 3 ...+... 4 ...+... 5 ...+... 6 ...+... 7 ...+... 8
 /COPY CTLWDMP
FTIMEOUT CF  E                      WORKSTN       KINFDS WSDS
F                                                 KNUM        1
 /COPY ERRDS
 /COPY PGMSDS
 /COPY STDTYPES
 /COPY WSCONS
 /COPY WSCUA
 /COPY WSDS
 *
 *
C          *ENTRY    PLIST
C                    PARM            TOEXIT
 *   Stay in program until Exit or Cancel is pressed, or
 *   until SCREEN1 format times-out.
 *
 *
 * Assume TimeOutExit is false
C                    MOVEL*OFF      TOEXIT
 *
 * Set first screen to SCREEN1
C                    MOVEL'SCREEN1' CURSCR  8 P
 *
C                    MOVEL*OFF      EXTPGM
C          EXTPGM    DOWEQ*OFF
 *
 * Read and write a screen
C                    EXSR WRTSCR
C                    READ TIMEOUT                 9899
 *
C                    SELEC
 * Handle EXIT keypress
C          WSKEY     WHEQ EXIT
C                    MOVEL*ON       EXTPGM
 *
 * Handle CANCEL keypress
C          WSKEY     WHEQ CANCEL
C                    MOVEL*ON       EXTPGM
 *
 * Handle screen time-out
C          WSSTAT    WHEQ WSTO
 * End program if current screen is SCREEN1
C          CURSCR    IFEQ 'SCREEN1'
C                    MOVEL*ON       TOEXIT
C                    MOVEL*ON       EXTPGM
C                    ENDIF
 *
C                    ENDSL
 *
 * Set next screen to display
C                    EXSR SETSCR
 *
C                    ENDDO
 *
C                    MOVEL*ON       *INLR
```

continued

FIGURE 15.2 CONTINUED

```
... 1 ...+... 2 ...+... 3 ...+... 4 ...+... 5 ...+... 6 ...+... 7 ...+... 8
C                     RETRN
 *
 *
 *--------------------------------------------------------------------
 * WRTSCR - Write a screen
 *--------------------------------------------------------------------
C           WRTSCR    BEGSR
C                     SELEC
 * Display screen format based on CURSCR field
C           CURSCR    WHEQ 'SCREEN1'
C                     WRITESCREEN1
 *
C           CURSCR    WHEQ 'SCREEN2'
C                     WRITESCREEN2
C                     ENDSL
 *
C                     ENDSR
 *
 *
 *--------------------------------------------------------------------
 * SETSCR - Set next screen to display
 *--------------------------------------------------------------------
C           SETSCR    BEGSR
 *
C                     SELEC
 *
 * Follow SCREEN1 with SCREEN2
C           CURSCR    WHEQ 'SCREEN1'
C                     MOVEL'SCREEN2' CURSCR       P
 *
 * Follow SCREEN2 with SCREEN1
C           CURSCR    WHEQ 'SCREEN2'
C                     MOVEL'SCREEN1' CURSCR       P
C                     ENDSL
 *
C                     ENDSR
 *
 *
 *--------------------------------------------------------------------
 * *INZSR - Initialize program variables at start-up
 *--------------------------------------------------------------------
C           *INZSR    BEGSR
 * Define ExitProgram var
C           *LIKE     DEFN #BOOL      EXTPGM
 * Define TimeOutExit var
C           *LIKE     DEFN #BOOL      TOEXIT
 *
C                     ENDSR
/COPY PSSR
```

For the RPG program you want to time-out, you need to specify a file feedback data structure for the WORKSTN file and provide one F-spec continuation line. The file feedback data structure is specified with the WSDS member from Figure 10.1 (Chapter 10); its WSSTAT field provides the means to determine that a time-out has occurred. Specify the name of this file feedback structure, WSDS, following the INFDS keyword on the first line of the F-spec. The other F-spec continuation line provides the NUM keyword, which specifies the number of devices defined for the associated WORKSTN file. For screen time-out purposes, you'll always use 1 for this value (don't worry, your operators will be able to successfully use concurrent copies of this program). In addition to including the WSDS member, also include the WSCONS and WSCUA members (Figures 10.2 and 10.4, respectively) from Chapter 10 (for the named constants they provide). Note also that while not absolutely necessary, this program includes the CTLWDMP, ERRDS, PGMSDS, and PSSR members for enhanced error-handling.

All that's necessary now is to provide your RPG program with what it needs to interpret and react to a time-out situation. To do this, immediately after each display file READ operation (be sure to specify an error indicator in columns 56–57), check the value of the WSSTAT field. If the value is 1331 (which is defined by the WSCONS member with the named constant WSTO), a time-out will have occurred (i.e., the time you specified with the WAITRCD parameter has expired and control has been automatically returned to your program). You can use the WSSTAT field to condition any code necessary to end your program, or perhaps to cause it to redisplay the previously displayed format. Note that this technique requires the WRITE/READ combination; the EXFMT operation will not work.

The example RPG program in Figure 15.2 shows a way to track which screen format is currently displayed (using the CURSCR variable), and how you can vary what time-out action occurs for different formats. This program also uses one input/output parameter (TOEXIT), whose purpose is to convey to the calling program whether or not a time-out condition caused the program to end. If that was the case, you might want the CL that called this program to sign off the workstation, for security purposes. By calling QCMDEXC, you could even take such drastic measures from within the timed-out program, but you'll probably find that it is better to let the calling CL program manage any additional time-out action required.

Chapter 16

Basic String Operations

Although RPG/400 has acquired a few string operations over the years (e.g., SUBST and SCAN), its built-in string handling capabilities are still quite meager. This and the next three chapters provide RPG string-handling functions that substantially enhance RPG's built-in string capabilities.

As with most of the RPG code presented in this book, our string-handling routines are provided in a "building-block" style. By using these cut-and-paste routines, you can quickly and easily work with strings in your RPG programs. This chapter provides what we consider "basic" string operations. The string functions not only provide consistent feedback of errors but also avoid the factor cram associated with RPG's string operations. Our basic string operations include determining the logical length of a string, determining the length of a string with *x* trailing blanks added, determining the length of a string with trailing blanks removed, and converting the case of an entire string. Subsequent chapters provide more complex string operations (see Appendix B for an interactive program to test the 12 string functions presented in this and the following three chapters).

The first two members, STRDS and STDCONST (Figures 16.1 and 16.2), provide the data structures and named constants our string-handling routines require. Use the /COPY directive to include these two members somewhere in your program's I-specs for any program that uses our string-handling routines.

FIGURE 16.1

STRDS RPG /COPY Member (Data Structures for String Functions)

```
... 1 ...+... 2 ...+... 3 ...+... 4 ...+... 5 ...+... 6 ...+... 7 ...+... 8
*-------------------------------------------------------------------------
* STRDS - Data structures for string functions
*
* Function:
*    Defines data structures for String functions.
*
* STR1DS   - str1_DS:
*    STR1   - str1_data
*    STR1LN - str1_len
*    STR1PS - str1_pos
*    STR1SZ - str1_size
*
* STR2DS   - str2_DS:
*    STR2   - str2_data
```

continued

FIGURE **16.1** *CONTINUED*

```
... 1 ...+... 2 ...+... 3 ...+... 4 ...+... 5 ...+... 6 ...+... 7 ...+... 8
*    STR2LN - str2_len
*    STR2PS - str2_pos
*    STR2SZ - str2_size
*
* STR3DS  - str3_DS:
*    STR3  - str3_data
*    STR3LN - str3_len
*    STR3PS - str3_pos
*    STR3SZ - str3_size
*
* STRVDS  - str_var_DS:
*    STRP   - str_ptr
*    STRERR - str_err
*    STRSIZ - str_size
*-------------------------------------------------------------------------
ISTR1DS    IDS
I                                        1 256 STR1
I                                      P 257 2580STR1LN
I                                      P 257 2580S1L
I                                      P 259 2600STR1PS
I                                      P 259 2600S1P
I                                      P 261 2620STR1SZ
I                                      P 261 2620S1S
*
ISTR2DS    IDS
I                                        1 256 STR2
I                                      P 257 2580STR2LN
I                                      P 257 2580S2L
I                                      P 259 2600STR2PS
I                                      P 259 2600S2P
I                                      P 261 2620STR2SZ
I                                      P 261 2620S2S
*
ISTR3DS    IDS
I                                        1 256 STR3
I                                      P 257 2580STR3LN
I                                      P 257 2580S3L
I                                      P 259 2600STR3PS
I                                      P 259 2600S3P
I                                      P 261 2620STR3SZ
I                                      P 261 2620S3S
*
ISTRVDS    IDS
I                                      P   1  20STRP
I                                          3   3 STRERR
I               256                    C        STRSIZ
*
```

FIGURE **16.2**
STDCONST RPG /COPY Member (Standard Named Constants)

```
... 1 ...+... 2 ...+... 3 ...+... 4 ...+... 5 ...+... 6 ...+... 7 ...+... 8
*-------------------------------------------------------------------------
* STDCONST - Standard named constants
*
* Function:
*   Defines standard named constants for use in any program.
*
```

continued

FIGURE **16.2** CONTINUED

```
... 1 ...+... 2 ...+... 3 ...+... 4 ...+... 5 ...+... 6 ...+... 7 ...+... 8
* Standard constants:
*    BLK     - blank
*    DGTC    - digit_chars
*    DPC     - dec_pos_chars
*    DPDGT   - dec_pos_digit
*    DPMSK   - dec_pos_mask
*    EOSTR   - end_of_string
*    MINUS   - minus_sign
*    PLUS    - plus_sign
*    SGNC    - numeric_sign_chars
*    UPRC    - upper_case_chars
*    LWRC    - lower_case_chars
*---------------------------------------------------------------------
I                   ' '                 C        BLK
I                   '0123456789'        C        DGTC
I                   '.'                 C        DPC
I                   '9'                 C        DPDGT
I                   .999999999          C        DPMSK
I                   X'00'               C        EOSTR
I                   '-'                 C        MINUS
I                   '+'                 C        PLUS
I                   '+-'                C        SGNC
I                   'ABCDEFGHIJKLMNOPQRST-C       UPRC
I                   'UVWXYZ'
I                   'abcdefghijklmnopqrst-C       LWRC
I                   'uvwxyz'
*
```

Member STRDS defines two string work fields, STR1 and STR2, which are each 256 characters long (the maximum-length RPG string field). Other numeric fields (e.g., string lengths, string positions, and string sizes) are also included in STRDS and associated with STR1 and STR2 to report the results of string operations (these fields all begin with STR, S1, or S2 prefixes). As you probably know, RPG doesn't support dynamically sized strings; rather, all strings are hard-coded to a given length. However, these string functions have been designed to mimic dynamically sized strings, using a 256-byte work field named STR1 to contain the results of the string functions. After using these string functions to modify the value in STR1, you can move that work field back into the target fields of your RPG programs.

DETERMINING A FIELD'S LOGICAL DATA LENGTH

The STRLEN routine (Figure 16.3) returns the logical length of data in a string field up to the right-most, non-blank character in that string (see Chapter 20 for a technique to determine the physical length of any field).

FIGURE 16.3
STRLEN RPG /COPY Member
(Returns the Logical Length of a String)

```
... 1 ...+... 2 ...+... 3 ...+... 4 ...+... 5 ...+... 6 ...+... 7 ...+... 8
*----------------------------------------------------------------------
* STRLEN - Length of string function
*
* Function:
*   Returns the length of data in a string up to the last
*   non-blank character.
*
* Requires copy modules:
*   STRDS    - Data structure for string functions.
*   STDCONST - Standard named constants.
*
* Expects:
*   STR1     - String value for which to determine logical length
*
* Returns:
*   STR1LN   - Logical length of STR1.
*   STRERR   - Error indicator (always *OFF).
*
* Example:
*   Find the length of the data in a string TEXT, and store
*   the answer in TEXTLN.
*
C*                      MOVELTEXT      STR1        P
C*                      EXSR STRLEN
C*                      Z-ADDSTR1LN    TEXTLN
*----------------------------------------------------------------------
C           STRLEN      BEGSR
*
C                       MOVE *OFF       STRERR
*
C           BLK         CHEKRSTR1       STR1LN
*
C                       ENDSR
*
```

To use the STRLEN function, use the /COPY directive to include this function somewhere in the subroutine portion of your RPG program's C-specs. STRLEN requires that the STRDS and STDCONST members (provided earlier in this chapter) also be included.

STRLEN expects

- STR1 to contain the string for which the length is desired

STRLEN returns

- STR1LN with the logical length of STR1 (i.e., if a field is defined as 12 characters long and contains the left-justified value "BOB," its logical length is 3)
- STRERR with the error condition

Before calling STRLEN, use the MOVEL operation to move your target field into the STR1 work field. Don't forget to use the P opcode extender with the MOVEL operations when you move source values to STR1 or STR2. The P opcode extender forces the target field to blanks before the move is performed. If you forget the P opcode extender, it's possible to have leftover string contents remain in STR1, which would cause the string functions to return the wrong results.

All our string-handling routines use the STRERR field to report errors to the calling code fl if an error occurs, STRERR will be set to 1; if not, STRERR will be set to 0. (Remember that 1 and 0 may also be represented by RPG's *ON and *OFF figurative constants, respectively). The STRLEN routine is a simple wrapper around RPG's CHEKR opcode, and STRLEN won't ever report an error. However, for syntactical consistency with our other string operations, the STRLEN function sets the STRERR field to *OFF — indicating an error did not occur when the STRLEN function was being executed.

For example, you could use the following code to determine the logical length of the data in the 32-byte TEXT field:

```
I/COPY STRDS
I/COPY STDCONST
       :
* Set source field to the value 'Test'
C                     MOVEL'Test'   TEXT     32 P
   :
C                     MOVELTEXT     STR1        P
C                     EXSR STRLEN
C                     Z-ADDSTR1LN   TEXTLN
```

After you use this code, the TEXTLN field contains the value 4. STRLEN isn't much value when used alone; but as you'll soon see, the information it provides about a string field can be used very effectively by our other string-handling routines.

PADDING A STRING WITH TRAILING BLANKS

The STRPAD function (Figure 16.4) returns the length of a string padded with a specified number of trailing blanks.

FIGURE 16.4
STRPAD RPG /COPY Member
(Returns the Length of a String Padded with *x* Blanks)

```
... 1 ...+... 2 ...+... 3 ...+... 4 ...+... 5 ...+... 6 ...+... 7 ...+... 8
*-------------------------------------------------------------------
* STRPAD - Pad string with trailing blanks function
*
* Function:
*    Returns the length of a string padded with x blanks, up to
*    the specified size. Returns an error if string length or
```

continued

FIGURE **16.4** CONTINUED

```
... 1 ...+... 2 ...+... 3 ...+... 4 ...+... 5 ...+... 6 ...+... 7 ...+... 8
 *   padded size is out of bounds.
 *
 * Requires copy modules:
 *   STRDS    - Data structure for string functions.
 *   STDCONST - Standard named constants.
 *
 * Expects:
 *   STR1     - String to pad.
 *   STR1LN   - Logical size of STR1.
 *   STR1SZ   - Trailing blanks to add.
 *
 * Returns:
 *   STR1LN   - Length of STR1 with padded blanks.
 *   STRERR   - Error indicator.
 *
 * Example:
 *   Pad a string TEXT, of length TEXTLN, with one blank
 *   separator before concatenating another string.
 *
 *                   MOVELTEXT    STR1      P
 C*                  Z-ADDTEXTLN  STR1LN
 C*                  Z-ADD1       STR1SZ
 C*                  EXSR STRPAD
 *
 C*        STRERR    IFEQ *OFF
 C*                  MOVELSTR1    TEXT      P
 C*                  Z-ADDSTR1LN  TEXTLN
 C*                  ELSE
 *                   :
 C                   ENDIF
 *-------------------------------------------------------------------
 C         STRPAD    BEGSR
 *
 C                   MOVE *OFF    STRERR
 *
 * Set new string length
 *
 C         STR1LN    ADD  STR1SZ  STRP
 *
 * Pad with trailing blanks when no errors
 *
 C                   SELEC
 *
 C         STRP      WHGT STRSIZ
 C         STR1LN    ORGT STRSIZ
 C         STR1SZ    ORGT STRSIZ
 C                   MOVE *ON     STRERR
 *
 C                   OTHER
 C                   Z-ADDSTRP    STR1LN
 *
 C                   ENDSL
 *
 C                   ENDSR
 *
```

An error is returned if the source string length or the padded size is out of bounds (for example, an error occurs if you try to pad a 132-character string with 132 blanks because the padded string would be greater than the 256-byte string fields that RPG/400 provides). To use the STRPAD function, use the /COPY directive to include this function somewhere in the subroutine portion of your RPG program's C-specs. STRPAD requires that the STRDS and STD-CONST members (provided earlier in this chapter) also be included.

STRPAD expects

- STR1 to contain the value of the string to pad
- STR1LN to contain the logical length of STR1
- STR1SZ to contain the number of blanks with which to pad STR1

STRPAD returns

- STR1LN with the new logical length of the padded string
- STRERR with error results

Here is an example of using the STRPAD function to pad a salutation field with one trailing blank:

```
I/COPY STRDS
I/COPY STDCONST
    :
* Set source field to the value 'Ms.'
C                   MOVEL'Ms.'   SALUTE  8 P
    :
C                   MOVELSALUTE  STR1      P
C                   Z-ADD3       STR1LN
C                   Z-ADD1       STR1SZ
C                   EXSR STRPAD
C                   Z-ADDSTR1LN  PADLEN
```

The new logical padded length of STR1 is returned in STR1LN. As you can see, this example isn't too effective because the logical length of the salutation is hard-coded. However, the STRLEN function can be used to remove this hard-coded dependency:

```
I/COPY STRDS
I/COPY STDCONST
    :
* Set source field to the value 'Ms.'
C                   MOVEL'Ms.'   SALUTE  8 P
    :
C                   MOVELSALUTE  STR1      P
C                   EXSR STRLEN
C                   Z-ADD1       STR1SZ
C                   EXSR STRPAD
C                   Z-ADDSTR1LN  PADLEN
```

This code would now return the new length of the padded string, regardless of the logical length of the salutation field.

TRIMMING TRAILING BLANKS FROM A STRING
The STRTRM function (Figure 16.5) returns the length of a string with trailing blanks removed, up to a maximum string length.

FIGURE 16.5
STRTRM RPG /COPY Member (Trim Trailing Blanks from a String)

```
... 1 ...+... 2 ...+... 3 ...+... 4 ...+... 5 ...+... 6 ...+... 7 ...+... 8
*------------------------------------------------------------------------
* STRTRM - Trim trailing blanks from string function
*
* Function:
*   Returns the length of a string with trailing blanks removed
*
* Requires copy modules:
*   STRDS    - Data structure for string functions
*   STDCONST - Standard named constants
*
* Expects:
*   STR1     - String value to trim
*   STR1LN   - Maximum length of trimmed string.
*
* Returns:
*   STR1LN   - Length of trimmed string.
*   STRERR   - Error indicator.
*
* Example:
*   Return length of string TEXT with trailing blanks
*   removed, with minimum length of TEXTLN.
C*                    MOVELTEXT      STR1      P
C*                    Z-ADDTEXTLN    STR1LN
C*                    EXSR STRTRM
C*                    MOVELSTR1      TEXT      P
C*                    Z-ADDSTR1LN    TEXTLN
*------------------------------------------------------------------------
C         STRTRM      BEGSR
*
C                     MOVE *OFF      STRERR
*
* Set position of last non-blank
*
C         BLK         CHEKRSTR1      STRP
*
* Trim trailing blanks when no errors
*
C                     SELEC
*
C         STR1LN      WHGT STRSIZ
C         STR1LN      ORLT STRP
C                     MOVE *ON       STRERR
*
C                     OTHER
C                     Z-ADDSTRP      STR1LN
*
C                     ENDSL
*
C                     ENDSR
*
```

An error occurs if the string length is out of bounds or if the length of the trimmed string exceeds the specified maximum length. To use the STRTRM function, use the /COPY directive to include this function somewhere in the subroutine portion of your RPG program's C-specs. STRTRM requires that the STRDS and STDCONST members (provided earlier in this chapter) also be included.

STRTRM expects

- STR1 to contain the string value to trim.
- STR1LN to contain the maximum size for the trimmed string. If the length of the trimmed string exceeds this value, an error is returned.

STRTRM returns

- STR1LN with the length of the trimmed string
- STRERR with error results

The following example reports the trimmed length of the TEXT field, assuming a maximum trimmed value of 32:

```
I/COPY STRDS
I/COPY STDCONST
   :
C                     MOVELTEXT      STR1       P
C                     Z-ADD32        STR1LN
C                     EXSR STRTRM
C           STRERR    IFEQ *ON
C                        trimmed string longer than maximum
C                     ELSE
C                        OK to use STR1LN value
C                     END
```

CONVERTING THE CASE OF A STRING

The STRLWR and STRUPR functions (Figures 16.6 and 16.7) convert the case of a string to either lowercase or uppercase.

FIGURE 16.6
STRLWR RPG /COPY Member (Convert a String to Lowercase)

```
... 1 ...+... 2 ...+... 3 ...+... 4 ...+... 5 ...+... 6 ...+... 7 ...+... 8
*-----------------------------------------------------------------------
* STRLWR - Convert string to lowercase function
*
* Function:
*   Convert a string to lowercase characters.
*
* Requires copy modules:
*   STRDS    - Data structure for string functions.
*   STDCONST - Standard named constants.
*
* Expects:
*   STR1     - String to convert to lowercase.
*
* Returns:
*   STR1     - String converted to lowercase.
*   STRERR   - Error indicator (always *OFF).
```

continued

FIGURE 16.6 *CONTINUED*

```
... 1 ...+... 2 ...+... 3 ...+... 4 ...+... 5 ...+... 6 ...+... 7 ...+... 8
 *
 * Example:
 *   Convert a string TEXT to lowercase.
 *
C*                      MOVELTEXT    STR1       P
C*                      EXSR STRLWR
C*                      MOVELSTR1    TEXT       P
 *-------------------------------------------------------------------------
C            STRLWR     BEGSR
 *
C                       MOVE *OFF    STRERR
 *
 * Convert to lowercase
 *
C            UPRC:LWRC XLATESTR1     STR1
 *
C                       ENDSR
```

FIGURE 16.7

STRUPR RPG /COPY Member (Convert a String to Uppercase)

```
... 1 ...+... 2 ...+... 3 ...+... 4 ...+... 5 ...+... 6 ...+... 7 ...+... 8
 *-------------------------------------------------------------------------
 * STRUPR - Convert string to uppercase function
 *
 * Function:
 *   Convert a string to uppercase characters.
 *
 * Requires copy modules:
 *   STRDS    - Data structure for string functions.
 *   STDCONST - Standard named constants.
 *
 * Expects:
 *   STR1     - String to convert to uppercase.
 *
 * Returns:
 *   STR1     - String converted to uppercase.
 *   STRERR   - Error indicator (always *OFF).
 *
 * Example:
 *   Convert a string TEXT to uppercase.
 *
C*                      MOVELTEXT    STR1       P
C*                      EXSR STRUPR
C*                      MOVELSTR1    TEXT       P
 *-------------------------------------------------------------------------
C            STRUPR     BEGSR
 *
C                       MOVE *OFF    STRERR
 *
 * Convert to uppercase
 *
C            LWRC:UPRC XLATESTR1     STR1
 *
C                       ENDSR
```

Both functions work in a similar way, so this discussion focuses only on the STRLWR function. To use the STRLWR or STRUPR functions, use the /COPY directive to include them somewhere in the subroutine portion of your RPG program's C-specs. STRLWR and STRUPR require that the STRDS and STD-CONST members (provided earlier in this chapter) also be included.

STRLWR expects

- STR1 to contain the string to convert to lowercase

STRLWR returns

- STR1 with the input string converted to lowercase
- STRERR with error results

The following example converts the string TEXT to all lowercase:

```
I/COPY STRDS
I/COPY STDCONST
   :
C                    MOVELTEXT      STR1      P
C                    EXSR STRLWR
C                    MOVELSTR1      TEXT      P
```

Before it calls STRLWR, the source string TEXT is moved into the work field STR1; upon return from STRLWR, the converted source string is moved into the source field TEXT. Note that, like the STRLEN function, the STRLWR and STRUPR functions don't need to check for errors. Thus, they unconditionally return *OFF in the STRERR field for syntactical consistency with our other string functions.

Chapter 17

Substring and String Concatenation Operations

This chapter presents two useful string operations: string concatenation (the ability to join two strings together) and substringing (the ability to extract a part of a string). While RPG offers the basic functionality of these operations with its SUBST and CAT opcodes, you'll find that these functions provide more robust error handling and a few extra features.

EXTRACTING A PART OF A STRING

The STRSUB routine (Figure 17.1) presents a robust alternative to RPG's SUBST opcode for performing substring operations. STRSUB provides built-in error trapping and lets you easily extract a substring value from a given location in the source string up to the end of the source string.

FIGURE 17.1
STRSUB RPG /COPY Member (Extract Substring Function)

```
... 1 ...+... 2 ...+... 3 ...+... 4 ...+... 5 ...+... 6 ...+... 7 ...+... 8
*-----------------------------------------------------------------------
* STRSUB - Substring function
*
* Function:
*   Extract a substring of the specified position and size
*   from a string. Returns an error if position or size is
*   out of bounds.
*
* Requires copy modules:
*   STRDS    - Data structure for string functions.
*   STDCONST - Standard named constants.
*   STRLEN   - Determine logical length of string.
*
* Expects:
*   STR1   - String from which to extract a value.
*   STR1PS - Starting position of substring in STR1.
*   STR1SZ - Size of substring. If this value is 256
*            (STRSIZ), then a substring starting at STR1PS
*            up to the logical end of the string is returned.
*
* Returns:
*   STR1   - Substring value.
*   STR1LN - Substring length.
*   STRERR - Error indicator. Returns an error if string position
*            or string size is out of bounds.
*
```

continued

FIGURE 17.1 CONTINUED

```
... 1 ...+... 2 ...+... 3 ...+... 4 ...+... 5 ...+... 6 ...+... 7 ...+... 8
* Example:
*   Extract a WORD from a string TEXT, of length TEXTLN,
*   of 8 characters starting in position 11.
*
C*                    MOVELTEXT     STR1       P
C*                    Z-ADD11       STR1PS
C*                    Z-ADD8        STR1SZ
C*                    EXSR STRSUB
 *
C*         STRERR     IFEQ *OFF
C*                    MOVELSTR1     WORD       P
C*                    Z-ADDSTR1LN   WORDLN
C*                    ELSE
 *                    :
C                     ENDIF
 *-----------------------------------------------------------------------
C          STRSUB     BEGSR
 *
C                     MOVE *OFF     STRERR
 *
* Set substring length if requested to end of string
 *
C          STR1SZ     IFEQ STRSIZ
C                     EXSR STRLEN
C          STR1LN     SUB  STR1PS   STR1SZ
C                     ADD  1        STR1SZ
C                     END
 *
* Set substring end position
 *
C          STR1PS     ADD  STR1SZ   STRP
C                     SUB  1        STRP
 *
* Substring when no errors
 *
C                     SELEC
 *
C          STR1PS     WHLT 1
C          STR1PS     ORGT STRSIZ
C          STR1SZ     ORGT STRSIZ
C          STRP       ORGT STRSIZ
C                     MOVE *ON      STRERR
 *
C                     OTHER
C                     Z-ADDSTR1SZ   STR1LN
C                     Z-ADDSTR1PS   STRP
C          STR1SZ     SUBSTSTR1:STRP STR1      P
 *
C                     ENDSL
 *
C                     ENDSR
```

To use the STRSUB function, use the /COPY directive to include this function somewhere in the subroutine portion of your RPG program's C-specs. STRSUB requires that the STRDS and STDCONST members, and the STRLEN function, also be included (see Chapter 16 for a discussion of these).

STRSUB expects

- STR1 to contain the source string from which you want to extract a substring.
- STR1PS to contain the starting position of the substring in STR1.
- STR1SZ to contain the size of substring desired. Setting STR1SZ to 256 causes the substring returned to start at the position specified and end at the logical end of the source string.

STRSUB returns

- STR1 with the extracted substring.
- STR1LN with the logical length of the extracted substring.
- STRERR with the error condition. An error is returned and the substring operation isn't performed if the substring starting position or substring size is out of bounds.

For example, to extract an 8-byte string from the TEXT field, starting at position 11, you would use the following code:

```
C                    MOVELTEXT      STR1      P
C                    Z-ADD11        STR1PS
C                    Z-ADD8         STR1SZ
C                    EXSR STRSUB
 *
C         STRERR     IFEQ *OFF
C                    MOVELSTR1      WORD      P
C                    Z-ADDSTR1LN    WORDLN
 * WORD now contains the extracted substring and WORDLN
 * contains the logical length of the substring.
C                    ELSE
     :               Error occurred

C                    ENDIF
```

To extract a substring beginning at position 5 and continuing to the end of the source string, you would use

```
I/COPY STRDS
I/COPY STDCONST
     :
C                    MOVELTEXT      STR1      P
C                    Z-ADD5         STR1PS
C                    Z-ADDSTRSIZ    STR1SZ
C                    EXSR STRSUB
```

In this example, if TEXT contained the value "Love Potion #9", the value returned in STR1 would be "Potion #9". This example uses the STRSIZ named constant value to specify 256 as the size of the substring to return fl which indicates to STRSUB to return a substring from the starting position to the end of the string. STRSIZ is defined in the STRDS member (shown in Figure 16.1 in Chapter 16).

CONCATENATING STRINGS

The STRCAT function (Figure 17.2) concatenates, or joins, two string values. STRCAT is an alternative to RPG/400's CAT operation code; however, unlike CAT, STRCAT is able to include trailing blanks and detect truncation. CAT always excludes trailing blanks. To insert space separators between the strings being concatenated, you would use the STRPAD string function (presented in Chapter 16) in conjunction with the STRCAT function (this chapter ends with an example of this).

FIGURE 17.2

STRCAT RPG /COPY Member (Concatenate Strings Function)

```
... 1 ...+... 2 ...+... 3 ...+... 4 ...+... 5 ...+... 6 ...+... 7 ...+... 8
*-----------------------------------------------------------------------
* STRCAT - Concatenate strings function
*
* Function:
*    Concatenates one string to the end of another string.
*    To insert separator characters at the end of the first
*    string, use the Pad String function STRPAD before
*    concatenating the strings. Returns an error on truncation.
*
* Requires copy modules:
*    STRDS    - Data structure for string functions
*    STDCONST - Standard named constants
*    STRLEN   - Determine logical length of string.
*
* Expects:
*    STR1    - First string to concatenate.
*    STR1LN  - Length of STR1. Using STRSIZ (256) causes the logical
*              length of STR1 to be used.
*    STR2    - Second string to concatenate.
*    STR2LN  - Length of STR2. Using STRSIZ (256) causes the logical
*              length of STR2 to be used.
*
* Returns:
*    STR1    - Concatenated string.
*    STR1LN  - Length of concatenated string.
*    STRERR  - Error indicator. Returns an error if string truncation occurs
*              or if length of concatenated string would exceed 256.
*
* Example:
*    Concatenate a WORD, of length WORDLN, to the end of a
*    string TEXT, of length TEXTLN. To insert separator
*    characters between TEXT and WORD, use the STRPAD function
*    to pad TEXT with trailing blanks before concatenating
*    WORD.
*
C*                     MOVELTEXT    STR1      P
C*                     Z-ADDTEXTLN  STR1LN
C*                     MOVELWORD    STR2      P
C*                     Z-ADDWORDLN  STR2LN
C*                     EXSR STRCAT
*
C*          STRERR     IFEQ *OFF
C*                     MOVELSTR1    TEXT      P
C*                     Z-ADDSTR1LN  TEXTLN
C*                     ELSE
*                      ...
```

continued

FIGURE **17.2** *CONTINUED*

```
... 1 ...+... 2 ...+... 3 ...+... 4 ...+... 5 ...+... 6 ...+... 7 ...+... 8
C*                    ENDIF
*-----------------------------------------------------------------------------
C          STRCAT     BEGSR
 *
C                     MOVE *OFF    STRERR               .
 *
 * Use logical length of STR2?
 *
C          STR2LN     IFEQ STRSIZ
 * Save STR1 and STR1LN
C                     MOVELSTR1    STR3      P
C                     Z-ADDSTR1LN  STR3LN
 * Determine logical length of STR2
C                     MOVELSTR2    STR1      P
C                     EXSR STRLEN
 * Save length of STR2
C                     Z-ADDSTR1LN  STR2LN
 * Restore STR1 and STR1LN
C                     MOVELSTR3    STR1      P
C                     Z-ADDSTR3LN  STR1LN
C                     ENDIF
 *
 * Use logical length of STR1?
 *
C          STR1LN     IFEQ STRSIZ
C                     EXSR STRLEN
C                     ENDIF
 *
 * Set size of string
 *
C          BLK        CHEKRSTR1    STR1SZ
 *
 * Set separator chars and length
 *
C          STR1LN     SUB  STR1SZ  STRP
C                     ADD  STR2LN  STR1LN
 *
 * Concatenate strings when no errors
 *
C                     SELEC
 *
C          STRP       WHLT 0
C          STR1LN     ORGT STRSIZ
C          STR2LN     ORGT STRSIZ
C                     MOVE *ON     STRERR
 *
C                     OTHER
C                     CAT  STR2:STRP STR1
 *
C                     ENDSL
 *
C                     ENDSR
```

To use the STRCAT function, use the /COPY directive to include this function somewhere in the subroutine portion of your RPG program's C-specs. STRCAT requires that the STRDS and STDCONST members, and the STRLEN function, also be included (see Chapter 16 for a discussion of these).

STRCAT expects

- STR1 to contain the first string to concatenate
- STR1LN to contain the length of STR1; setting STR1LN to 256 causes the logical length of STR1 to be used
- STR2 to contain the second string to concatenate
- STR2LN to contain the length of STR2; setting STR2LN to 256 causes the logical length of STR2 to be used

STRCAT returns

- STR1 with the concatenated string values
- STR1LN with the logical length of the concatenated string
- STRERR with the error condition. An error is returned if string truncation would occur during concatenation or if the length of the concatenated string would exceed 256.

For example, if the field WORD1 contains the value "AS" and the field WORD2 contains the value "/400", the code

```
I/COPY STRDS
I/COPY STDCONST
   :
C                        MOVELWORD1      STR1        P
C                        Z-ADD2          STR1LN
C                        MOVELWORD2      STR2        P
C                        Z-ADD4          STR2LN
C                        EXSR STRCAT
```

would concatenate the two values, returning "AS/400" in the STR1 field, and "6" in the STR1LN field (the logical length of STR1).

Let's take a look at Figure 17.3, which uses the STRPAD function from Chapter 16 with this chapter's STRCAT function. This use of STRPAD shows how to add separator spaces for string concatenation. This example concatenates a city/state/Zip code string from three separate field values.

FIGURE 17.3

Concatenating a City/State/Zip Code String
from Three Separate Field Values

```
... 1 ...+... 2 ...+... 3 ...+... 4 ...+... 5 ...+... 6 ...+... 7 ...+... 8
I/COPY STRDS
I/COPY STDCONST
   :
I              'Indianapolis'      C        VCITY
I              'IN'                C        VSTATE
```

continued

FIGURE **17.3** *CONTINUED*

```
... 1 ...+... 2 ...+... 3 ...+... 4 ...+... 5 ...+... 6 ...+... 7 ...+... 8
I              '46992'                 C         VZIP
I              50                      C         CSZSIZ
   :
 * Set source field values.
C                    MOVELVCITY     CITY    32 P
C                    MOVELVSTATE    STATE    2 P
C                    MOVELVZIP      ZIP     10 P
C                    MOVEL*BLANKS   CSZ     50
 *
 * Concatenate city name with a comma and trailing space.
C                    MOVELCITY      STR1       P
C                    Z-ADDSTRSIZ    STR1LN
C                    MOVEL', '      STR2       P
C                    Z-ADD2         STR2LN
C                    EXSR STRCAT
 *
 * Concatenate state with STR1.
C                    MOVELSTATE     STR2
C                    Z-ADDSTRSIZ    STR2LN
C                    EXSR STRCAT
 *
 * Pad STR1 with three trailing blanks.
C                    EXSR STRLEN
C                    Z-ADD3         STR1SZ
C                    EXSR STRPAD
 *
 * Concatenate zipcode with STR1.
C                    MOVELZIP       STR2
C                    Z-ADDSTRSIZ    STR2LN
C                    EXSR STRCAT
 * STR1 now contains the left-justified value:
 * Indianapolis, IN   46992
 * and STR1LN contains 24, the logical length of
 * concatenated value in STR1.
 * Now, save the concatenated value in the
 * field named CSZ.
C          STRERR    IFEQ *OFF
C                    MOVELSTR1      CSZ        P
C                    ELSE
   :                 Error occurred
C                    ENDIF
```

Note that, in this example, the CITY, STATE, and ZIP fields are all concatenated using string lengths of STRSIZ (which is a named constant for the value 256) to cause the logical length of these fields to be used for string concatenation. Using this feature of STRCAT makes it easy to perform concatenation without regard for the string lengths. Note also how the STRPAD function is used to append three blank spaces to the string after the state name has been concatenated. Using STRPAD here is what causes the three blanks to appear between the state and the Zip code in the final concatenated result.

This example also illustrates how the STR1 value is used as a perpetual target for subsequent string operations. Knowing that the string functions used expect input in STR1 and return output in STR1, once it has set the initial value of STR1 (with the CITY field), this code simply uses the string functions to continually transform the value of STR1 until the desired results are achieved.

Chapter 18

Justifying and Centering Strings

This chapter provides three string functions for justifying string values. With these functions, which have no direct RPG/400 alternative, you can left- or right-justify a string and you can center a string.

RIGHT-JUSTIFYING A STRING

The STRRAJ function (Figure 18.1) right-justifies a string field. To use the STRRAJ function, use the /COPY directive to include this function somewhere in the subroutine portion of your RPG program's C-specs.

FIGURE 18.1
STRRAJ RPG /COPY Member (Right-Adjust a String)

```
... 1 ...+... 2 ...+... 3 ...+... 4 ...+... 5 ...+... 6 ...+... 7 ...+... 8
*-----------------------------------------------------------------------
* STRRAJ - Right-justify string function
*
* Function:
*   Right-justifies the data in a string within a specified
*   size. Returns an error if string length or adjusted size
*   is out of bounds.
*
* Requires copy modules:
*   STRDS    - Data structure for string functions
*   STDCONST - Standard named constants
*
* Expects:
*   STR1   - the string value to right-justify.
*   STR1SZ - the target length of the right-justified string.
*
* Returns:
*   STR1   - the string right-justified.
*   STR1LN - the logical length of the justified string.
*   STRERR - the error condition. An error is returned if the string
*            length or adjusted size is out of bounds.
*
* Example:
*   Right-justify the string TEXT within a string size of
*   80 characters.
*
C*                  MOVELTEXT      STR1      P
C*                  Z-ADD80        STR1SZ
C*                  EXSR STRRAJ
*
C*        STRERR    IFEQ *OFF
C*                  MOVELSTR1      TEXT      P
C*                  Z-ADDSTR1LN    TEXTLN
C*                  ELSE
*                   ...
```

continued

FIGURE **18.1** *CONTINUED*

```
... 1 ...+... 2 ...+... 3 ...+... 4 ...+... 5 ...+... 6 ...+... 7 ...+... 8
C*                    ENDIF
 *--------------------------------------------------------------------
C          STRRAJ    BEGSR
 *
C                    MOVE *OFF       STRERR
 *
 * Set position of last non-blank
 *
C          BLK       CHEKRSTR1       STRP
 *
 * Pad with leading blanks when no errors
 *
C                    SELEC
 *
C          STRP      WHGT STR1SZ
C          STR1SZ    ORGT STRSIZ
C                    MOVE *ON        STRERR
 *
C                    OTHER
C                    Z-ADDSTR1SZ     STR1LN
C          STR1SZ    SUB  STRP       STRP
C                    MOVE *BLANKS    STR2
C          STR2      CAT  STR1:STRP STR1
 *
C                    ENDSL
 *
C                    ENDSR
```

STRRAJ requires that the STRDS and STDCONST members (see Chapter 16) also be included.STRRAJ expects·STR1 to contain the string value to right-justify. STR1SZ to contain the target length of the right-justified string.

STRRAJ returns

- STR1 with the string right-justified
- STR1LN with the logical length of the justified string
- STRERR with the error condition; an error is returned if the string length or adjusted size is out of bounds

For example, to right-justify the string TEXT within a string size of 80 characters, you would use the following:

```
I/COPY STRDS
I/COPY STDCONST
       :
C                    MOVELTEXT       STR1         P
C                    Z-ADD80         STR1SZ
C                    EXSR STRRAJ
 *
C          STRERR    IFEQ *OFF
C                    MOVELSTR1       TEXT         P
C                    Z-ADDSTR1LN     TEXTLN
C                    ELSE
     :               Error occurred
C                    ENDIF
```

LEFT-JUSTIFYING A STRING

The STRLAJ function (Figure 18.2) left-justifies a string field. To use the STRLAJ function, use the /COPY directive to include this function somewhere in the subroutine portion of your RPG program's C-specs.

FIGURE 18.2

STRLAJ RPG /COPY Member (Left-Adjust a String)

```
... 1 ...+... 2 ...+... 3 ...+... 4 ...+... 5 ...+... 6 ...+... 7 ...+... 8
*-----------------------------------------------------------------------
* STRLAJ - Left-adjust string function
*
* Function:
*   Left-justifies the data in a string. Returns an error if
*   string length is out of bounds.
*
* Requires copy modules:
*   STRDS     - Data structure for string functions
*   STDCONST - Standard named constants
*
* Expects:
*   STR1   - the string value to left-justify.
*   STR1LN - the logical length of the source string (STR1) to justify.
*
* Returns:
*   STR1   - the string left-justified.
*   STR1LN - the logical length of the justified string.
*   STRERR - the error condition. An error is returned if the source
*            string length is out of bounds.
*
* Example:
*   Left-justify the data in a string TEXT, of length TEXTLN.
*
C*                    MOVELTEXT    STR1      P
C*                    Z-ADDTEXTLN  STR1LN
C*                    EXSR STRLAJ
*
C*         STRERR     IFEQ *OFF
C*                    MOVELSTR1    TEXT      P
C*                    ELSE
*                     ...
C*                    ENDIF
*
*-----------------------------------------------------------------------
C          STRLAJ     BEGSR
*
C                     MOVE *OFF     STRERR
*
* Set position of first non-blank
*
C          BLK        CHECKSTR1     STRP
*
* Trim leading blanks when no errors
*
C                     SELEC
*
C          STR1LN     WHGT STRSIZ
C          STR1LN     ORLT STRP
C                     MOVE *ON      STRERR
```

continued

FIGURE **18.2** CONTINUED

```
... 1 ...+... 2 ...+... 3 ...+... 4 ...+... 5 ...+... 6 ...+... 7 ...+... 8
     *
     * Trimming is only necessary when there are leading
     * blanks (i.e.- when STRP is greater than 1)
     *
C           STRP      WHGT 1
C           STR1LN    SUB  STRP      STR1SZ
C                     ADD  1         STR1SZ
C           STR1SZ    SUBSTSTR1:STRP STR1      P
C                     Z-ADDSTR1SZ    STR1LN
     *
C                     ENDSL
     *
C                     ENDSR
```

STRLAJ requires that the STRDS and STDCONST members also be included (see Chapter 16).

STRLAJ expects

- STR1 to contain the string value to left-justify
- STR1LN to contain the logical length of the source string (STR1) to justify

STRLAJ returns

- STR1 with the string left-justified
- STR1LN with the logical length of the justified string
- STRERR with the error condition; an error is returned if the source string length is out of bounds

For example, to left-justify the 40-character string TEXT, you would use the following:

```
I/COPY STRDS
I/COPY STDCONST
     :
C                         MOVELTEXT      STR1      P
C                         Z-ADD40        STR1LN
C                         EXSR STRLAJ
     *
C           STRERR        IFEQ *OFF
C                         MOVELSTR1      TEXT      P
C                         ELSE
     :                    Error occurred
C                         ENDIF
```

If you were unsure of the logical length of the source string, you could first call the STRLEN function (Chapter 16). For example,

```
I/COPY STRDS
I/COPY STDCONST
     :
C                         MOVELTEXT      STR1      P
```

```
C                      EXSR STRLEN
C                      EXSR STRLAJ
```

CENTERING A STRING

The STRCTR function (Figure 18.3) centers a string field. This function is handy for centering report and screen headings when they are passed as parameters to programs. To use the STRCTR function, use the /COPY directive to include this function somewhere in the subroutine portion of your RPG program's C-specs.

FIGURE 18.3

STRCTR RPG /COPY Member (Center a String)

```
... 1 ...+... 2 ...+... 3 ...+... 4 ...+... 5 ...+... 6 ...+... 7 ...+... 8
*---------------------------------------------------------------
* STRCTR - Center string function
*
* Function:
*   Center the data in a string within a specified size.
*   Returns an error if string length or centered size is out
*   of bounds.
*
* Requires copy modules:
*   STRDS    - Data structure for string functions
*   STDCONST - Standard named constants
*
* Expects:
*   STR1   - the string to center.
*   STR1LN - the logical length of the string to center
*            (the logical length of STR1).
*   STR1SZ - the centered string size.
*
* Returns:
*   STR1   - the centered string.
*   STR1LN - the length of the centered string (the value
*            specified for the STR1SZ parameter)
*   STRERR - the error condition. An error is returned if the
*            string length or centered size is out of bounds.
*
* Example:
*   Center a heading in the string HDG, of length HDGLN,
*   within a string size of 80 characters.
*
C*                MOVELHDG    STR1    P
C*                Z-ADDHDGLN  STR1LN
C*                Z-ADD80     STR1SZ
C*                EXSR STRCTR
*
C*       STRERR   IFEQ *OFF
C*                MOVELSTR1   HDG     P
C*                Z-ADDSTR1LN HDGLN
C*                ELSE
*                 ...
C*                ENDIF
*
*---------------------------------------------------------------
C        STRCTR   BEGSR
*
C                 MOVE *OFF    STRERR
```

continued

FIGURE **18.3** *CONTINUED*

```
... 1 ...+... 2 ...+... 3 ...+... 4 ...+... 5 ...+... 6 ...+... 7 ...+... 8
     *
     * Set position of first non-blank
     *
C           BLK         CHECKSTR1         STRP
     *
     * Trim leading blanks when no errors
     *
C                       SELEC
     *
C           STR1LN      WHGT STRSIZ
C           STR1SZ      ORGT STRSIZ
C           STRP        ORGT STR1LN
C                       MOVE *ON           STRERR
     *
C           STRP        WHGT 1
C                       SUB  STRP          STR1LN
C                       ADD  1             STR1LN
C           STR1LN      SUBSTSTR1:STRP STR1          P
     *
C                       ENDSL
     *
     * Center string when no error
     *
C           STRERR      IFEQ *OFF
C                       Z-ADDSTR1SZ        STR1LN
C           BLK         CHEKRSTR1          STRP
C           STR1SZ      SUB  STRP          STRP
C                       DIV  2             STRP
C                       MOVE *BLANKS       STR2
C           STR2        CAT  STR1:STRP STR1
C                       ENDIF
     *
C                       ENDSR
```

STRCTR requires that the STRDS and STDCONST members also be included (see Chapter 16).

STRCTR expects

- STR1 to contain the string to center
- STR1LN to contain the logical length of the string to center (the logical length of STR1)
- STR1SZ to contain the centered string size

STRCTR returns

- STR1 with the centered string
- STR1LN with the length of the centered string (the value specified for the STR1SZ parameter)
- STRERR with the error condition; an error is returned if the string length or centered size is out of bounds

For example, to center a report heading in the string HDG, of length 80, with a target centered size of 80 characters, you would use this code:

```
C                     MOVELHDG      STR1       P
C                     Z-ADD80       STR1LN
C                     Z-ADD80       STR1SZ
C                     EXSR STRCTR
 *
C          STRERR     IFEQ *OFF
C                     MOVELSTR1     HDG        P
C                     Z-ADDSTR1LN   HDGLN
C                     ELSE
    :
C                     ENDIF
```

Chapter 19

Searching Strings

RPG/400 provides a rudimentary string-searching function with its SCAN opcode. This chapter's string functions put robust, easy-to-use wrappers around SCAN. With these functions, you can easily search a string to find occurrences of a specified string value, starting from either the left or the right side of the searched string.

FINDING LEFTMOST OCCURRENCES OF A STRING VALUE

The STRFND function (Figure 19.1) finds the first occurrence (and, optionally, subsequent occurrences) of a specified value from the left side of a searched string. To use the STRFND function, use the /COPY directive to include this function somewhere in the subroutine portion of your RPG program's C-specs.

FIGURE 19.1

STRFND RPG /COPY Member (Find First Occurrence of a String)

```
... 1 ...+... 2 ...+... 3 ...+... 4 ...+... 5 ...+... 6 ...+... 7 ...+... 8
*---------------------------------------------------------------------
* STRFND - Find first occurrence of string function
*
* Function:
*    Finds the first occurrence of argument in a string,
*     starting at the specified position.
*
* Requires copy modules:
*    STRDS    - Data structure for string functions
*    STDCONST - Standard named constants
*
* Expects:
*    STR1   - String value to search.
*    STR1LN - Length of string value to search.
*    STR1PS - Starting position of search.
*    STR2   - Value to search for.
*    STR2LN - Length of value to search for.
*
* Returns:
*    STR1PS - Position of search value.
*    STRERR - Error indicator.
*
* Example:
*    Find the first occurrence of "The" in a string TEXT, of
*    length TEXTLN and store the position of the match in WRDPS.
*
C*                     MOVELTEXT       STR1      P
C*                     Z-ADDTEXTLN     STR1LN
C*                     Z-ADD1          STR1PS
C*                     MOVEL'The'      STR2      P
C*                     Z-ADD3          STR2LN
```

continued

FIGURE **19.1** *CONTINUED*

```
... 1 ...+... 2 ...+... 3 ...+... 4 ...+... 5 ...+... 6 ...+... 7 ...+... 8
C*                    EXSR STRFND
 *
C*         STRERR     IFEQ *OFF
C*                    Z-ADDSTR1PS    WRDPS
C*                    ELSE
 *                    ...
C*                    ENDIF
 *---------------------------------------------------------------------
C          STRFND     BEGSR
 *
C                     MOVE *OFF       STRERR
 *
 *  Set end position of shortest possible search result
 *
C          STR2LN     ADD  STR1PS     STRP
C                     SUB  1          STRP
 *
 * Find string when no errors
 *
C                     SELEC
 *
C          STR1PS     WHLT 1
C          STR1PS     ORGT STR1LN
C          STR1LN     ORGT STRSIZ
C          STR2LN     ORLT 1
C          STR2LN     ORGT STRSIZ
C          STRP       ORGT STRSIZ
C                     MOVE *ON        STRERR
 *
C                     OTHER
C          STR2:S2L   SCAN STR1:S1P   STRP
C                     Z-ADDSTRP       STR1PS
C          STRP       ADD  STR2LN     STRP
C                     SUB  1          STRP
C          STR1PS     IFEQ 0
C          STRP       ORGT STR1LN
C                     MOVE *ON        STRERR
C                     ENDIF
 *
C                     ENDSL
 *
C                     ENDSR
 *
```

STRFND requires that the STRDS and STDCONST members also be included (see Chapter 16).

STRFND expects

- STR1 to contain the string value to search
- STR1LN to contain the length of the string value to search
- STR1PS to contain the starting position of search1
- STR2 to contain the string value to search for
- STR2LN to contain the length of the value to search for

STRFND returns

- STR1PS with the position of the located search value
- STRERR with the error condition; an error is returned if the search value is not found

For example, if the 80-character field TEXT contained the value "The quick red fox", the following code would locate the first occurrence of "fox" in that string and put its location in the field WRDPS:

```
I/COPY STRDS
I/COPY STDCONST
   :
C                      MOVELTEXT      STR1      P
C                      Z-ADD80        STR1LN
C                      Z-ADD1         STR1PS
C                      MOVEL'fox'     STR2      P
C                      Z-ADD3         STR2LN
C                      EXSR STRFND
 *
C            STRERR    IFEQ *OFF
C                      Z-ADDSTR1PS    WRDPS
 * WRDPS now contains the value 15.
C                      ELSE
   :                   Search value wasn't found.
C                      ENDIF
```

Be careful how you specify search values when you use STRFND. For example, consider the field TEXT with the string value "this is a test" and the need to find the first occurrence of the word "is" in that field. At a glance, you might think the following code returns the value 6:

```
C                      MOVELTEXT      STR1      P
C                      Z-ADD80        STR1LN
C                      Z-ADD1         STR1PS
C                      MOVEL'is'      STR2      P
C                      Z-ADD2         STR2LN
C                      EXSR STRFND
```

However, after this code is performed, STR2LN doesn't contain the value 6; it contains the value 3 because it found the occurrence of "is" in the word "This". To avoid this problem, the search should have been specified as

```
C                      MOVELTEXT      STR1      P
C                      Z-ADD80        STR1LN
C                      Z-ADD1         STR1PS
C                      MOVEL' is'     STR2      P
C                      Z-ADD3         STR2LN
C                      EXSR STRFND
```

Note the leading blank that was added to the search value (STR2); also note that the search length (STR2LN) has been set to 3. This code returns the expected search results of 5.

Using a DOWHILE loop and incrementing the search position (STR1PS) each time a value is found, it's easy to iterate a string search across an entire string. For example, given the value "This is a test is a test is a test is a test is a test", the following code locates each occurrence of " is" in that string:

```
I/COPY STRDS
I/COPY STDCONST
     :
I                   'This is a test is -  C          VTEXT
I                   'a test is a test i-
I                   's a test is a test'
 *
C                       MOVELVTEXT      STR1        P
C                       EXSR STRLEN
C                       Z-ADD1          STR1PS
 *
C                       MOVEL' is'      STR2
C                       Z-ADD3          STR2LN
 *
 * Attempt to find first occurrence of ' is'
C                       EXSR STRFND
 *
C          STRERR    DOWNE*ON
     :
     : STR1PS now contains the location of an occurrence of '
       is'
     :
     :              Perform some code
     :
 * Bump search position to position immediately after
 * previous position found.
C                       ADD  1          STR1PS
 * Attempt search again.
C                       EXSR STRFND
C                       ENDDO
```

FINDING RIGHTMOST OCCURRENCES OF A STRING VALUE

The STRFNL function (Figure 19.2) finds the first occurrence (and, optionally, subsequent occurrences) of a specified value from the right side of a searched string. You'll probably use STRFND to find occurrences from the beginning of the string; but for those times when you need to search a string from end to beginning, STRFNL will come in handy. To use the STRFNL function, use the /COPY directive to include this function somewhere in the subroutine portion of your RPG program's C-specs.

FIGURE 19.2
STRFNL RPG /COPY Member (Find Last Occurrence of a String)

```
... 1 ...+... 2 ...+... 3 ...+... 4 ...+... 5 ...+... 6 ...+... 7 ...+... 8
*------------------------------------------------------------------------
* STRFNL - Find last occurrence of string function
*
* Function:
*   Finds the last occurrence of argument in a string,
*   ending at the specified position.
*
* Requires copy modules:
*   STRDS     - Data structure for string functions
*   STDCONST - Standard named constants
*   STRFND    - Find first occurrence of string function
*
* Expects:
*   STR1   - String value to search.
*   STR1LN - Length of string value to search.
*   STR1PS - Position at which to end search.
*   STR2   - Value to search for.
*   STR2LN - Length of value to search for.
*
* Returns:
*   STR1PS - Position of search value.
*   STRERR - Error indicator.
*
* Example:
*   Find the last occurrence of "The" in a string TEXT, of
*   length TEXTLN and store the position of the match in WRDPS.
*
C*                     MOVELTEXT      STR1      P
C*                     Z-ADDTEXTLN    STR1LN
C*                     Z-ADDTEXTLN    STR1PS
C*                     MOVEL'The'     STR2      P
C*                     Z-ADD3         STR2LN
C*                     EXSR STRFNL
*
C*          STRERR     IFEQ *OFF
C*                     Z-ADDSTR1PS    WRDPS
C*                     ELSE
*                      :
C*                     ENDIF
*
*------------------------------------------------------------------------
C           STRFNL     BEGSR
*
C           *LIKE      DEFN STR1PS    @FLSLP
C           *LIKE      DEFN STR1PS    @FLSSP
*
C                      MOVE *OFF      STRERR
*
* Find string while no errors
*
C                      Z-ADD0         @FLSSP
C                      Z-ADDSTR1PS    @FLSLP
C                      Z-ADD1         STR1PS
C                      EXSR STRFND
*
C           STRERR     DOWEQ*OFF
C           STR1PS     ANDLE@FLSLP
*
C                      Z-ADDSTR1PS    @FLSSP
C                      ADD  1         STR1PS
```

continued

FIGURE **19.2** *CONTINUED*

```
... 1 ...+... 2 ...+... 3 ...+... 4 ...+... 5 ...+... 6 ...+... 7 ...+... 8
C                   EXSR STRFND
 *
C                   ENDDO
 *
 * Search ok if string found before end position
 *
C           @FLSSP  IFGT 0
C           @FLSSP  ANDLE@FLSLP
C                   Z-ADD@FLSSP     STR1PS
C                   MOVE *OFF       STRERR
C                   ELSE
C                   Z-ADD0          STR1PS
C                   MOVE *ON        STRERR
C                   ENDIF
 *
C                   ENDSR
```

STRFND requires that the STRDS and STDCONST members (see Chapter 16), and the STRFNL function (provided earlier in this chapter) also be included.

STRFNL expects

- STR1 to contain the string value to search
- STR1LN to contain the length of the string value to search
- STR1PS to contain the right-most position at which the search ended
- STR2 to contain the value to search for
- STR2LN to contain the length of the value to search for

STRFNL returns

- STR1PS with the position of the located search value
- STRERR with the error condition; an error is returned if the search value is not found

For example, given the value "This is a test is a test is a test is a test is a test", the following code locates the last occurrence of " is" in that string:

```
I/COPY STRDS
I/COPY STDCONST
      :
I                   'This is a test is - C           VTEXT
I                   'a test is a test i-
I                   's a test is a test'
 *
C                   MOVELVTEXT      STR1        P
C                   EXSR STRLEN
C                   Z-ADDSTR1LN     STR1PS
 *
C                   MOVEL' is'      STR2
C                   Z-ADD3          STR2LN
C                   EXSR STRFNL
```

```
 *
C            STRERR    IFEQ *OFF
C                      Z-ADDSTR1PS    WRDPS
 * WRDPS now contains the value 45.
C                      ELSE
   :5                     Search value wasn't found.
C                      ENDIF
```

Note the use of the STRLEN function (from Chapter 16's Figure 16.3) to dynamically determine the length of the string being searched. To ensure that the last occurrence of " is" is found, that same value is also used as the position at which to end the search. Had the value of STR1PS been set to anything less than 45 (ending the search just before the last occurrence of " is"), STRFNL would have returned 35, the location of the next-to-the-last occurrence of " is" in the searched string.

Chapter 20

Determining the Size of a Field

Use the techniques in this chapter to dynamically determine the length of any field and the number of decimal places in a numeric field.

For some coding techniques, you may need to know the declared size of a field. For example, to use the OS/400 APIs to edit a numeric field, you need to know the length and number of decimal places in the field. Or for dynamically building a string to display in a subfile (to provide a horizontal "panning" feature, for example), you'll need to know the length of each field being used. You could just hard-code these values; but when field sizes change, you have a maintenance nightmare. A much better approach is to dynamically determine field attributes at runtime using the following modules:

FLDLEN   provides a template for determining the size of any field (Figure 20.1)

FLDDP   provides a routine for determining the number of decimal places in a numeric field (Figure 20.2)

FIGURE 20.1
FLDLEN Length of Field Template

```
... 1 ...+... 2 ...+... 3 ...+... 4 ...+... 5 ...+... 6 ...+... 7 ...+... 8
*------------------------------------------------------------------------
* FLDLEN    Length of field template
*
* Function:
*   Return the declared length of a field. This function
*   replaces the value of the field. Save and restore the
*   field to preserve its value.
*
* Usage:
*   Copy this template into your program and replace all
*   &values listed below with your actual program variables.
*
* Requires copy modules:
*   STRDS      Data structure for string functions
*   STDCONST   Standard named constants
*   STRLEN     Length of string function
*
* Expects:
*   &fld       field
*   &len       field_len
*------------------------------------------------------------------------
C                   MOVE *ZEROS     &fld
C                   MOVEL&fld       STR1      P
C                   EXSR STRLEN
C                   Z-ADDSTR1LN     &len
```

FIGURE 20.2
FLDDP Decimal Positions in Numeric Field Function

```
... 1 ...+... 2 ...+... 3 ...+... 4 ...+... 5 ...+... 6 ...+... 7 ...+... 8

*-------------------------------------------------------------------------
* FLDDP    Decimal positions in numeric field function
*
* Function:
*   Return the decimal positions in a numeric field. This
*   function replaces the value of the field. Save and restore
*   the field to preserve its value.
*
* Requires copy module:
*   STDCONST    Standard named constants
*
* Expects:
*   DPTST   - dec_pos_test containing the value of field after
*             DPMSK (dec_pos_mask) assigned to field
*
* Returns:
*   DP      - dec_pos
*
* Example:
*   Calculate the number of decimal places in an amount field
*   AMT and store the answer in AMTDP. Uses SVAMT to save the
*   value of AMT.
*
C*          *LIKE       DEFN AMT       SVAMT
C*                      Z-ADDAMT       SVAMT
*
C*                      Z-ADDDPMSK     AMT
C*                      Z-ADDAMT       DPTST
C*                      EXSR FLDDP
C*                      Z-ADDDP        AMTDP   30
*
C*                      Z-ADDSVAMT     AMT
*
*-------------------------------------------------------------------------
C           FLDDP       BEGSR
*
C                       Z-ADDDPTST     DPTST   99
C                       MOVELDPTST     aDPTST 10 P
*
C           DPDGT       CHECKaDPTST    DP
C                       SUB  1         DP      30
*
C                       ENDSR
```

You will also need the STRDS, STRLEN, and STDCONST members from Chapter 16.

To determine the length of a field, add /COPY statements for STRDS and STDCONST at the end of the I-specs, and /COPY statements for STRLEN at the end of the C-specs. Then copy the FLDLEN template into your program and replace &fld with the name of the field and &len with a 3-digit numeric field to hold the length of &fld. To store the length of ORDAMT in AMTLEN, you would use the code

```
C                         MOVE *ZEROS   ORDAMT
C                         MOVELORDAMT   STR1       P
C                         EXSR STRLEN
C                         Z-ADDSTR1LN   AMTLEN
```

Determining the number of decimal places in a numeric field is just as easy. Add /COPY statements for STDCONST at the end of the I-specs, and /COPY statements for FLDDP at the end of the C-specs. To find the number of decimal places in ORDAMT and store the answer in AMTDP, you code

```
C                         Z-ADDDPMSK    ORDAMT
C                         Z-ADDORDAMT   DPTST
C                         EXSR FLDDP
C                         Z-ADDDP       AMTDP    30
```

Notice that both the techniques shown above overwrite the contents of a field. You can generally avoid problems caused by overwriting field contents by determining field sizes in your *INZSR initialization routine. If you use these routines in your code's mainline or in other subroutines, be sure to save field contents so that the contents can be restored after you use these routines.

Chapter 21

Editing Numeric Fields

With these two simple routines, you can edit any numeric value within an RPG program for output to a character field.

For most types of output, you can use edit codes on RPG O-specs or in a display file's DDS to edit numeric values. But suppose you want to embed an edited number in a string of text, or transfer numeric values to a remote system that doesn't support OS/400 data types. If you're ever faced with this kind of problem, try using the following /COPY modules:

EDTDS   provides the EDTDS data structure for editing a number (Figure 21.1)

EDTINZ   initializes an edit mask for a numeric field (Figure 21.2)

EDTNBR   edits a numeric field using the edit mask created by EDTINZ (Figure 21.3)

FIGURE 21.1

EDTDS Data Structure for Edit Function

```
... 1 ...+... 2 ...+... 3 ...+... 4 ...+... 5 ...+... 6 ...+... 7 ...+... 8
 *-----------------------------------------------------------------------
 * EDTDS    Data structure for Edit function
 *
 * Function:
 *   Defines parameters and constants for Edit functions.
 *
 * EDTDS -  edit_API_DS:
 *   EDTMSK - edit_mask
 *   EDTARG - edit_args:
 *     EDTMLN - edit_mask_len
 *     EDTSLN - edit_str_len
 *     EDTFIL - edit_fill_char
 *     EDTCDE - edit_code
 *     EDTFLT - edit_float_char
 *     EDTVLN - edit_var_len
 *     EDTVDP - edit_var_dec_pos
 *   EDTVAR - edit_var
 *   EDTCLS - edit_var_class
 *   EDTSTR - edit_str
 *-----------------------------------------------------------------------
IEDTDS      IDS
I                                      1 256 EDTMSK
 *
I                                    257 275 EDTARG
I                                  B 257 2600EDTMLN
I                                  B 261 2640EDTSLN
I                                    265 265 EDTFIL
I                                    266 266 EDTCDE
I                                    267 267 EDTFLT
I                                  B 268 2710EDTVLN
I                                  B 272 2750EDTVDP
```

continued

FIGURE 21.1 CONTINUED

```
... 1 ...+... 2 ...+... 3 ...+... 4 ...+... 5 ...+... 6 ...+... 7 ...+... 8
 *
I                                       276 2900EDTVAR
I I            '*ZONED'                 291 300 EDTCLS
I                                       301 364 EDTSTR
```

FIGURE 21.2

EDTINZ Initialize Numeric Edit Function

```
... 1 ...+... 2 ...+... 3 ...+... 4 ...+... 5 ...+... 6 ...+... 7 ...+... 8
*-----------------------------------------------------------------------------
* EDTINZ    Initialize numeric edit function
*
* Function:
*   Initializes the edit mask and arguments required by the
*   Edit Number function EDTNBR. The edit mask may be created
*   for any valid RPG edit code. Use the Field Length and
*   Decimal Positions functions FLDLEN and FLDDP to obtain
*   the declared size of the numeric field.
*
* Requires copy modules:
*   EDTDS     Data structure for Edit functions
*   ERRDS     Error data structure returned by APIs
*
* Expects:
*   EDTCDE - edit_code
*   EDTVLN - edit_var_len
*   EDTVDP - edit_var_dec_pos
*   EDTFLT - edit_float_char
*
* Returns:
*   EDTMSK - edit_mask
*   EDTARG - edit_args:
*     EDTMLN - edit_mask_len
*     EDTSLN - edit_str_len
*     EDTFIL - edit_fill_char
*   ERRDS  - err_API_DS
*
* Example:
*   Initialize the edit mask AMTMSK and the edit arguments
*   AMTARG for an amount field AMT, which is to be edited
*   using the "L" edit code. The length and decimal positions
*   in AMT have been calculated using the FLDLEN and FLDDP
*   functions and stored in AMTLN and AMTDP.
*
C*           *LIKE     DEFN EDTMSK     AMTMSK
C*           *LIKE     DEFN EDTARG     AMTARG
*
C*                     MOVE 'L'        EDTCDE
C*                     Z-ADDAMTLN      EDTVLN
C*                     Z-ADDAMTDP      EDTVDP
C*                     EXSR EDTINZ
C*                     MOVE EDTMSK     AMTMSK
C*                     MOVE EDTARG     AMTARG
*
*-----------------------------------------------------------------------------
C           EDTINZ    BEGSR
*
C                     CALL 'QECCVTEC'
```

continued

FIGURE **21.2** *CONTINUED*

```
... 1 ...+... 2 ...+... 3 ...+... 4 ...+... 5 ...+... 6 ...+... 7 ...+... 8
C                      PARM           EDTMSK
C                      PARM           EDTMLN
C                      PARM           EDTSLN
C                      PARM           EDTFIL
C                      PARM           EDTCDE
C                      PARM           EDTFLT
C                      PARM           EDTVLN
C                      PARM           EDTVDP
C                      PARM           ERRDS
 *
 * Clear optional arguments
 *
C                      MOVE *BLANKS   EDTFLT
 *
C                      ENDSR
```

FIGURE **21.3**
EDTNBR Edit Number Function

```
... 1 ...+... 2 ...+... 3 ...+... 4 ...+... 5 ...+... 6 ...+... 7 ...+... 8
 *-------------------------------------------------------------------------
 * EDTNBR - Edit number function
 *
 * Function:
 *   Edits a number using the edit mask and arguments created
 *   by the Initialize Edit function EDTINZ.
 *
 * Requires copy modules:
 *   EDTDS  - Data structure for Edit functions
 *   ERRDS  - Error data structure returned by APIs
 *   INZEDT - Initialize numeric edit function
 *
 * Expects:
 *   EDTVAR - edit_var
 *   EDTMSK - edit_mask
 *   EDTARG - edit_args
 *
 * Returns:
 *   EDTSTR - edit_str
 *   ERRDS  - err_API_DS
 *
 * Example:
 *   Edit an amount field AMT, using the edit mask AMTMSK and
 *   edit arguments AMTARG created by EDTINZ, and store the
 *   edited value in the string AMTSTR.
 *
C*                     MOVELAMT       EDTVAR
C*                     MOVE AMTMSK    EDTMSK
C*                     MOVE AMTARG    EDTARG
C*                     EXSR EDTNBR
C*                     MOVELEDTSTR    AMTSTR 32 P
 *
 *-------------------------------------------------------------------------
C         EDTNBR       BEGSR
 *
C                      MOVE *BLANKS   EDTSTR
 *
```

continued

FIGURE 21.3 CONTINUED

```
... 1 ...+... 2 ...+... 3 ...+... 4 ...+... 5 ...+... 6 ...+... 7 ...+... 8
C                   CALL 'QECEDT'
C                   PARM           EDTSTR
C                   PARM           EDTSLN
C                   PARM           EDTVAR
C                   PARM           EDTCLS
C                   PARM           EDTVLN
C                   PARM           EDTMSK
C                   PARM           EDTMLN
C                   PARM           EDTFIL
C                   PARM           ERRDS
 *
C                   ENDSR
```

You will also need the ERRDS module shown in Figure 2.2 of Chapter 2. To use the modules, you code /COPY statements for the ERRDS and EDTDS data structures at the end of the I-specs, and /COPY statements for EDTINZ and EDTNBR at the end of the C-specs.

The routines provided in this chapter harness two OS/400 APIs, QECCVTEC and QECEDT. To edit a numeric value, first you use the EDTINZ routine (which calls the QECCVTEC API) to translate any valid RPG edit code into an edit mask for a particular numeric field. An edit mask is an overlay that is used to edit a field. It's best to execute EDTINZ from the *INZSR subroutine in your program so that it only runs once for each field you want to edit. Please note that EDTINZ needs to know the length and number of decimal places in the field you want to edit: Instead of hard-coding these values, look at the FLDLEN and FLDDP routines in Chapter 20 to see how to determine them dynamically at runtime.

To initialize the edit mask for the order amount in ORDAMT, of length AMTLEN with decimal places AMTDP, which is to be edited using the "L" edit code, you code

```
C           *LIKE     DEFN EDTMSK    AMTMSK
C           *LIKE     DEFN EDTARG    AMTARG
 *
C                     MOVE 'L'       EDTCDE
C                     Z-ADDAMTLEN    EDTVLN
C                     Z-ADDAMTDP     EDTVDP
C                     EXSR EDTINZ
C                     MOVE EDTMSK    AMTMSK
C                     MOVE EDTARG    AMTARG
```

The EDTINZ routine returns two values: an edit mask that is saved in AMTMSK, and a set of editing arguments that is saved in AMTARG.

Once the edit mask has been created, you can use it as many times as you want to edit the ORDAMT field by adding the following code to execute the EDTNBR routine (which calls the QECEDT API):

```
C                     MOVELORDAMT    EDTVAR     P
C                     MOVE AMTMSK    EDTMSK
C                     MOVE AMTARG    EDTARG
C                     EXSR EDTNBR
C                     MOVELEDTSTR    AMTSTR 32 P
```

The edited value returned by the routine is stored in AMTSTR. The snippet of code above sizes AMTSTR larger than needed so that it contains enough room for the largest value ORDAMT can hold, with additional space for any edit characters inserted by the edit mask, such as a sign, commas, or a decimal point.

When you are using the EDTNBR function, it's important to remember that this function works just like the editing in your RPG O-specs or DDS. If the edit code you use specifies zero supression, then leading zeros in the output field will be replaced by blanks. If you want to concatenate the output into a text string, you will want to remove the leading blanks. For an easy way to do this, see the STRTRM function in Chapter 16, which trims leading blanks from a string.

Chapter 22

Reformatting Numeric Data

Use this routine to translate a numeric value in a string into a numeric field.

Client/server applications are often complicated by the incompatibility between the data types allowed on the client and server platforms. You may find your AS/400 receives numeric data from a client, such as a PC or an RS/6000, in an edited format that includes a sign and embedded decimal point, rather than in the signed-numeric format with assumed decimal point you are used to. For this situation, you need a routine for converting such edited data into numeric values you can process in your RPG programs. The NBRFMT routine presented in this chapter (Figure 22.1) does just that. NBRFMT accepts a string that contains an edited number and converts that edited number to a numeric field. To use NBRFMT, you will also need the STDCONST /COPY module from Chapter 16.

FIGURE 22.1
NBRFMT Format Number from String Function

```
... 1 ...+... 2 ...+... 3 ...+... 4 ...+... 5 ...+... 6 ...+... 7 ...+... 8
 *--------------------------------------------------------------------------
 * NBRFMT    Format number from string function
 *
 *
 * Function:
 *    Formats a number from a string that may include leading
 *    and trailing blanks, a leading or trailing sign, an
 *    integer value, a decimal point, and decimal places. Use
 *    the Field Length and Decimal Positions functions FLDLEN
 *    and FLDDP to obtain the declared size of the field.
 *
 * Requires copy modules:
 *    STDCONST   Standard named constants
 *
 * Expects:
 *    NBRSTR  - number_str
 *    NBRLEN  - number_len
 *    NBRDP   - number_dec_pos (optional)
 *    NBRSGN  - number_signed (optional)
 *
 * Returns:
 *    NBR     - number
 *    NBRERR  - number_error
 *
 * Example:
 *    Format an amount field AMT from a string AMTSTR. The
 *    length and decimal positions in AMT have been calculated
 *    using the FLDLEN and FLDDP functions and stored in AMTLN
```

continued

FIGURE 22.1 *CONTINUED*

```
... 1 ...+... 2 ...+... 3 ...+... 4 ...+... 5 ...+... 6 ...+... 7 ...+... 8
 *    and AMTDP. AMT may be signed.
 *
C*                       MOVELAMTSTR     NBRSTR      P
C*                       Z-ADDAMTLN      NBRLEN
C*                       Z-ADDAMTDP      NBRDP
C*                       MOVE *ON        NBRSGN
C*                       EXSR NBRFMT
 *
C*          NBRERR       IFEQ *OFF
C*                       MOVE NBR        AMT
C*                       ELSE
 *                       ...
C*                       ENDIF
 *
 *---------------------------------------------------------------------------
C           NBRFMT       BEGSR
 *
 * Declare variables
 *
C                        Z-ADD0          NBR     150
C                        MOVE NBRLEN     NBRLEN   30
C                        MOVE NBRDP      NBRDP    30
C                        MOVE NBRSGN     NBRSGN    1
C                        MOVE NBRSTR     NBRSTR   32
C                        MOVE *OFF       NBRERR    1
 *
C                        MOVELNBRSTR     @NSTR    33
C                        MOVE EOSTR      @NSTR
C                        Z-ADD33         @NEOS    30
C                        MOVE *ZEROS     @NNBR    15
C                        Z-ADD15         @NSIZ    30
C                        Z-ADD1          @NP      30
C                        Z-ADD1          @NN      30
C                        Z-ADD0          @NI      30
C                        MOVE *BLANKS    @NINT    32
C                        Z-ADD0          @ND      30
C                        MOVE *ZEROS     @NDEC    32
C                        MOVE *BLANKS    @NSGN     1
 *
 * A number may include leading and trailing blanks, leading or
 * trailing sign, integers, decimal point, and decimals.
 *
 * Bypass leading blanks
 *
C                        Z-ADD@NN        @NP
C           BLK          CHECK@NSTR:@NP  @NN
 *
 * Check for leading sign
 *
C                        Z-ADD@NN        @NP
C           SGNC         CHECK@NSTR:@NP  @NN
C           @NN          IFGT @NP
C           1            SUBST@NSTR:@NP  @NSGN
C           @NP          ADD  1          @NN
C                        ENDIF
 *
 * Check for integers
 *
C                        Z-ADD@NN        @NP
C           DGTC         CHECK@NSTR:@NP  @NN
```

continued

FIGURE 22.1 *CONTINUED*

```
... 1 ...+... 2 ...+... 3 ...+... 4 ...+... 5 ...+... 6 ...+... 7 ...+... 8
C              @NN        IFGT @NP
C              @NN        SUB  @NP        @NI
C              @NI        SUBST@NSTR:@NP @NINT
C                         ENDIF
 *
 * Check for decimal point
 *
C                         Z-ADD@NN        @NP
C              DPC        CHECK@NSTR:@NP @NN
C              @NN        IFGT @NP
C              @NP        ADD  1          @NN
C                         ENDIF
 *
 * Check for decimals
 *
C                         Z-ADD@NN        @NP
C              DGTC       CHECK@NSTR:@NP @NN
C              @NN        IFGT @NP
C              @NN        SUB  @NP        @ND
C              @ND        SUBST@NSTR:@NP @NDEC
C                         ENDIF
 *
 * Check for trailing sign
 *
C              @NSGN      IFEQ *BLANKS
C                         Z-ADD@NN        @NP
C              SGNC       CHECK@NSTR:@NP @NN
C              @NN        IFGT @NP
C              1          SUBST@NSTR:@NP @NSGN
C              @NP        ADD  1          @NN
C                         ENDIF
C                         ENDIF
 *
 * Bypass trailing blanks
 *
C                         Z-ADD@NN        @NP
C              BLK        CHECK@NSTR:@NP @NN
 *
 * Error if next pointer not at end of string
 *
C              @NN        IFNE @NEOS
C                         MOVE *ON        NBRERR
C                         ENDIF
 *
 * Error if length out of range or integer truncation, or
 * not signed and negative, but allow decimal truncation
 *
C              NBRLEN     SUB  NBRDP      @NP
C              NBRLEN     IFLT 1
C              NBRLEN     ORGT @NSIZ
C              NBRLEN     ORLT NBRDP
C              @NI        ORGT @NP
C              NBRSGN     ORNE *ON
C              @NSGN      ANDEQMINUS
C                         MOVE *ON        NBRERR
C                         ENDIF
 *
 * Format number when no errors found
 *
C              NBRERR     IFEQ *OFF
 *
```

continued

FIGURE **22.1** CONTINUED

```
... 1 ...+... 2 ...+... 3 ...+... 4 ...+... 5 ...+... 6 ...+... 7 ...+... 8
C           @NSIZ     SUB  NBRDP      @NP
C                     SUB  @NI        @NP
C           @NP       IFNE 0
C           @NP       SUBST@NNBR:1    @NNBR      P
C                     ELSE
C                     CLEAR@NNBR
C                     ENDIF
C                     CAT  @NINT:0    @NNBR
C                     CAT  @NDEC:0    @NNBR
C                     MOVE @NNBR      NBR
C           @NSGN     IFEQ MINUS
C                     Z-SUBNBR        NBR
C                     ENDIF
 *
C                     ENDIF
 *
 * Clear optional arguments
 *
C                     Z-ADD0          NBRDP
C                     MOVE *OFF       NBRSGN
 *
C                     ENDSR
```

We've designed NBRFMT to be as simple as possible. The routine can accept a string of up to 32 characters, which can contain

- leading and trailing blanks
- an optional leading or trailing sign
- an integer value
- a decimal point
- a decimal value

The routine can reformat this string as a number up to 15 digits long. The routine checks for invalid numeric data and integer truncation, and returns an error if either occurs. Just like the edit routines in the previous chapter, NBRFMT needs to know the length and number of decimal places in the number to be formatted. Although you could hard-code these values, we strongly recommend you use the FLDLEN and FLDDP routines in Chapter 20 to dynamically determine them at runtime.

To use NBRFMT, you add a /COPY statement for STDCONST at the end of your I-specs, and a /COPY statement for NBRFMT at the end of the C-specs. To reformat the value in AMTSTR into signed-numeric field ORDAMT, of length AMTLEN with decimal places AMTDP, you code

```
C                     MOVELAMTSTR     NBRSTR     P
C                     Z-ADDAMTLEN     NBRLEN
C                     Z-ADDAMTDP      NBRDP
C                     MOVE *ON        NBRSGN
C                     EXSR NBRFMT
 *
```

```
C           NBRERR    IFEQ *OFF
C                     MOVE NBR       ORDAMT
C                     ELSE
   :                  handle error
C                     ENDIF
```

NBRFMT returns the number into NBR, which is then moved to ORDAMT. The decimal places in NBRDP and the sign in NBRSGN are optional; both can be omitted when not required, to simplify the reformatting of unsigned integer fields.

Chapter 23

Reformatting Dates

Use these modules to reformat and validate dates.

After character and numeric variables, dates are the most commonly used data type in business applications. You will find homegrown routines in most programs for reformatting or validating dates. In this chapter, we show you a simple function for converting dates from one format to another. You can also use this function to validity-check date fields. The modules we present in this chapter are

DATDS	provides the DATDS data structure and named constants required by DATCNT and DATCVT (Figure 23.1)
DATCNT	returns the century indicator for a date (Figure 23.2)
DATCVT	uses the OS/400 QWCCVTDT API to convert a date from one format to another (Figure 23.3)

You will also need module ERRDS from Figure 2.2 of Chapter 2.

FIGURE 23.1
DATDS Data Structure for Date Functions

```
... 1 ...+... 2 ...+... 3 ...+... 4 ...+... 5 ...+... 6 ...+... 7 ...+... 8
*-----------------------------------------------------------------------
* DATDS    Data structure for Date functions
*
* Function:
*   Defines parameters and constants for Date functions.
*
* DATDS     date_DS:
*   DTFMTI   date_in_format
*   DTVARI   date_in_var:
*     DTCNTI   date_in_cent
*     DTDATI   date_in_date
*       DTJULI   date_in_julian
*     DTTIMI   date_in_time
*     DTMLSI   date_in_millisecs
*   DTFMTO   date_out_format
*   DTVARO   date_out_var:
*     DTCNTO   date_out_cent
*     DTDATO   date_out_date
*       DTJULO   date_out_julian
*     DTTIMO   date_out_time
*     DTMLSO   date_out_millisecs
*-----------------------------------------------------------------------
IDATDS      IDS
I                                       1  10 DTFMTI
I                                      11  26 DTVARI
I                                      11  11 DTCNTI
I                                      12  17 DTDATI
```

continued

FIGURE 23.1 CONTINUED

```
... 1 ...+... 2 ...+... 3 ...+... 4 ...+... 5 ...+... 6 ...+... 7 ...+... 8
I                                         12  16 DTJULI
I                                         18  23 DTTIMI
I                                         24  26 DTMLSI
 *
I                                         27  36 DTFMTO
I                                         37  52 DTVARO
I                                         37  37 DTCNTO
I                                         38  43 DTDATO
I                                         38  42 DTJULO
I                                         44  49 DTTIMO
I                                         50  52 DTMLSO
 *
 *----------------------------------------------------------------------
 *    DTFCUR - date_fmt_curr_clock   cent, date, time, millisecs
 *    DTFDTS - date_fmt_time_stamp   cent, date, time, millisecs
 *    DTFJOB - date_fmt_job          cent, date
 *    DTFSYS - date_fmt_sys_val      cent, date
 *    DTFYMD - date_fmt_YMD          cent, date
 *    DTFMDY - date_fmt_MDY          cent, date
 *    DTFDMY - date_fmt_DMY          cent, date
 *    DTFJUL - date_fmt_julian       cent, julian
 *    DTC20  - date_cent_20
 *    DTC21  - date_cent_21
 *----------------------------------------------------------------------
I              '*CURRENT '           C         DTFCUR
I              '*DTS     '           C         DTFDTS
I              '*JOB     '           C         DTFJOB
I              '*SYSVAL  '           C         DTFSYS
I              '*YMD     '           C         DTFYMD
I              '*MDY     '           C         DTFMDY
I              '*DMY     '           C         DTFDMY
I              '*JUL     '           C         DTFJUL
I              '0'                   C         DTC20
I              '1'                   C         DTC21
```

FIGURE 23.2

DATCNT Return Century Indicator for Date Function

```
... 1 ...+... 2 ...+... 3 ...+... 4 ...+... 5 ...+... 6 ...+... 7 ...+... 8
 *-----------------------------------------------------------
 * DATCNT    Return century indicator for date function
 *
 * Function:
 *   Return the century indicator for a date. The date must be
 *   in YMD format. Returns DTC20 for the 20th century if the
 *   year is greater than 39, else DTC21 for the 21st century.
 *
 * Requires copy modules:
 *   DATDS  - Data structure for Date functions
 *
 * Expects:
 *   DTDATI - date_in_date (in YMD format)
 *
 * Returns:
 *   DTCNTO - date_out_cent
 *   DTERR  - date_err on error
 *
```

continued

FIGURE **23.2** *CONTINUED*

```
... 1 ...+... 2 ...+... 3 ...+... 4 ...+... 5 ...+... 6 ...+... 7 ...+... 8
 * Example:
 *   Return the century indicator for the current date in CURDAT
 *   and store the result in CURCNT.
 *
C*          *LIKE     DEFN DTCNTO   CURCNT
 *
C*                    MOVE CURDAT   DTDATI
C*                    EXSR DATCNT
C*                    MOVE DTCNTO   CURCNT
 *
 *------------------------------------------------------------------------
C           DATCNT    BEGSR
 *
C                     MOVE *OFF     DTERR    1
C                     MOVE @DTPOS   @DTPOS   30
 *
C           DGTC      CHECKDTDATI   @DTPOS
 *
C                     SELEC
 *
C           @DTPOS    WHNE 0
C                     MOVE *ON      DTERR
 *
C           DTDATI    WHGE '400000'
C                     MOVE DTC20    DTCNTO
 *
C                     OTHER
C                     MOVE DTC21    DTCNTO
 *
C                     ENDSL
 *
C                     ENDSR
```

FIGURE **23.3**

DATCVT Convert Date Function

```
... 1 ...+... 2 ...+... 3 ...+... 4 ...+... 5 ...+... 6 ...+... 7 ...+... 8
 *------------------------------------------------------------------------
 * DATCVT    Convert date function
 *
 * Function:
 *   Convert a date from one format to another. See the named
 *   constants at the end of copy member DATDS for the possible
 *   formats. The date must have an associated century code.
 *   Use the Retrieve Century function DATCNT for dates that
 *   do not have a century code.
 *
 * Requires copy modules:
 *   DATDS  - Data structure for Date functions
 *   ERRDS  - Error data structure returned by APIs
 *
 * Expects:
 *   DTFMTI - date_in_format
 *   DTVARI - date_in_var:
 *     DTCNTI - date_in_cent
 *     DTDATI - date_in_date
 *       DTJULI - date_in_julian
 *     DTTIMI - date_in_time
```

continued

FIGURE 23.3 CONTINUED

```
... 1 ...+... 2 ...+... 3 ...+... 4 ...+... 5 ...+... 6 ...+... 7 ...+... 8
*      DTMLSI - date_in_millisecs
*    DTFMTO - date_out_format
*
* Returns:
*    DTVARO - date_out_var:
*       DTCNTO - date_out_cent
*       DTDATO - date_out_date
*       DTJULO - date_out_julian
*       DTTIMO - date_out_time
*       DTMLSO - date_out_millisecs
*    DTERR  -  date_err on error
*    ERRDS  -  err_API_DS describing error
*
* Example:
*   Convert the current date in CURDAT, of century CURCNT,
*   from YMD format to Julian format, and store the result
*   in CURJUL.
*
C*                     MOVE CURCNT    DTCNTI
C*                     MOVE CURDAT    DTDATI
C*                     MOVE DTFYMD    DTFMTI
C*                     MOVE DTFJUL    DTFMTO
C*                     EXSR DATCVT
*
C*          DTERR      IFEQ *OFF
C*                     MOVE DTCNTO    CURCNT
C*                     MOVE DTJULO    CURJUL
C*                     ELSE
*                      ...
C*                     ENDIF
*
*--------------------------------------------------------------------------
C           DATCVT     BEGSR
*
C                      MOVE *OFF      DTERR   1
*
C                      CALL 'QWCCVTDT'
C                      PARM           DTFMTI
C                      PARM           DTVARI
C                      PARM           DTFMTO
C                      PARM           DTVARO
C                      PARM           ERRDS
*
C           ERRDLN     IFGT Ø
C                      MOVE *ON       DTERR
C                      ENDIF
*
C                      ENDSR
```

To use the modules, you include the ERRDS and DATDS data structures at the end of the I-specs. The DATDS module (Figure 23.1) defines the input and output variables for the DATCVT function (Figure 23.3) and the date formats that DATCVT supports. All date formats require a century indicator as well as a date: Use named constant DTC20 (or '0') for the twentieth century; use named constant DTC21 (or '1') for the twenty-first century. For dates without an associated century indicator, you can use the DATCNT function (Figure 23.2) to return a century indicator. DATCNT expects dates in year-month-day format and returns DTC20 for years 40–99, or DTC21 for years 00–39.

To return a century indicator for an order date, ORDDAT, add a /COPY statement for the DATCNT module at the end of the C-specs, and then code

```
C               *LIKE      DEFN DTCNTO      ORDCNT
  *
C                          MOVE ORDDAT      DTDATI
C                          EXSR DATCNT
C                          MOVE DTCNTO      ORDCNT
```

Once a date field has an associated century indicator, you can use the DATCVT function (Figure 23.3) to convert it into any format. To convert ORDDAT from year-month-day (DTFYMD) to your system format (DTFSYS), add a /COPY statement for the DATCVT module at the end of the C-specs, and then code

```
C                          MOVE ORDCNT      DTCNTI
C                          MOVE ORDDAT      DTDATI
C                          MOVE DTFYMD      DTFMTI
C                          MOVE DTFSYS      DTFMTO
C                          EXSR DATCVT
  *
C               DTERR      IFEQ *OFF
C                          MOVE DTCNTO      ORDCNT
C                          MOVE DTDATO      ORDDAT
C                          ELSE
    :                      handle error here

C                          ENDIF
```

The DATCVT function returns an error field, DTERR, if the input date is invalid. As a result, you can use DATCVT to validate date fields as well as to convert them. For example, if your order-entry program accepts an order date from a display file in system format (DTFSYS), you code the following to validate and convert it to DTFYMD format:

```
C                          MOVE DTC20       DTCNTI
C                          MOVE ORDDAT      DTDATI
C                          MOVE DTFSYS      DTFMTI
C                          MOVE DTFYMD      DTFMTO
C                          EXSR DATCVT
  *
C               DTERR      IFEQ *OFF
C                          MOVE DTDATO      ORDDAT
C                          MOVE ORDDAT      DTDATI
C                          EXSR DATCNT
C                          MOVE DTCNTO      ORDCNT
C                          ELSE
    :                      handle error here

C                          ENDIF
```

Notice how we use DTC20 as dummy input for DATCVT, and then use DATCNT to return the actual century indicator for ORDDAT once it is in year-month-day format. This technique allows the user to enter a 6-character date, from which the program calculates the corresponding century indicator.

We should point out one limitation to the DATCVT function. The QWC-CVTDT API used by the subroutine only supports century indicators for the twentieth and twenty-first centuries. We haven't found any problems with this approach; but if your system stores dates outside this range, say for a catalog of old master paintings, you will have to use another technique for reformatting dates that supports a full 4-digit year.

Chapter 24

Doing Date Arithmetic

Learn the basics of date arithmetic with two simple programs: ZDATADD adds or subtracts a number of days from a date; ZDATDIF calculates the difference in days between two dates.

Date arithmetic is an absolute must for many applications. An inventory application needs to add the lead time for a product to the purchase order date to find the expected receipt date. For sales order processing, you may want to analyze performance by looking at the difference between the actual and planned shipment dates for each order. In this chapter, we show you two programs for solving these problems; but first we'll explain the design of our date arithmetic routines. This background knowledge will not only help you understand the code but will also give you the basics for writing your own date routines.

The main problem with dates is finding some universal format in which they can be manipulated. Because the date routines in the previous chapter support dates in the twentieth and twenty-first century, we decided to convert dates into days, taking January 1, 1900, as our base point, or day 1. We knew that once dates were in this universal format, date arithmetic would be easy. To add days to a date, convert the date to universal format, add the days, then convert back to Gregorian format. To find the difference between two dates, convert the dates to universal format, then subtract one from the other.

To simplify the conversion from Gregorian to universal format, we decided to split the process into two steps. We first use the DATCVT routine from the previous chapter to convert from year-month-day to a Julian date, which consists of a 2-digit year, followed by a 3-digit day in the year. Then we use the DATJ2U routine (Figure 24.1) to convert from Julian to universal format.

FIGURE 24.1
DATJ2U Convert Date from Julian to Universal Format Functions

```
... 1 ...+... 2 ...+... 3 ...+... 4 ...+... 5 ...+... 6 ...+... 7 ...+... 8
*-------------------------------------------------------------------
* DATJ2U   Convert date from Julian to Universal format function
*
* Function:
*   Convert a date from Julian format to Universal format. The
*   Universal format is the number of days since 1st Jan 1900.
*   Use the Convert Date function DATCVT to convert the input
*   date to Julian format if required.
*
* Requires copy modules:
```

continued

FIGURE 24.1 *CONTINUED*

```
... 1 ...+... 2 ...+... 3 ...+... 4 ...+... 5 ...+... 6 ...+... 7 ...+... 8
 *    DATDS   -    Data structure for Date functions
 *    STDCONST - Standard named constants
 *
 * Expects:
 *    DTVARI - date_in_var:
 *      DTCNTI - date_in_cent
 *      DTJULI - date_in_julian
 *
 * Returns:
 *    DTDATO - date_out_date in Universal format
 *    DTERR  - date_err on error
 *
 * Example:
 *    Convert the current Julian date in CURJUL, of century
 *    CURCNT, into Universal format and store the result in
 *    CURUDT.
 *
C*                      MOVE CURCNT      DTCNTI
C*                      MOVE CURJUL      DTJULI
C*                      EXSR DATJ2U
C*                      MOVE DTDATO      CURUDT
 *
 *-------------------------------------------------------------------
C           DATJ2U      BEGSR
 *
C                       MOVE *OFF        DTERR    1
C                       MOVE @DTPOS      @DTPOS   30
C                       MOVE @DTUNV      @DTUNV   60
C                       MOVE @DTCYR      @DTCYR   30
C                       MOVE @DTDAY      @DTDAY   30
 *
C           DGTC        CHECKDTJULI      @DTPOS
 *
 * If no errors, split into century/year and day in year, then
 * convert to Universal format
 *
C                       SELEC
 *
C           @DTPOS      WHNE 0
C           DTCNTI      ORLT '0'
C           DTCNTI      ORGT '1'
C                       MOVE *ON         DTERR
 *
C                       OTHER
C                       MOVELDTVARI      @DTCYR
C                       MOVE DTJULI      @DTDAY
C           @DTCYR      SUB  1           @DTUNV
C                       MULT 365.25      @DTUNV
C                       ADD  365         @DTUNV
C                       ADD  @DTDAY      @DTUNV
C                       MOVE @DTUNV      DTDATO
 *
C                       ENDSL
 *
C                       ENDSR
```

To convert from universal back to Gregorian, we just reverse the process. First convert from universal to Julian using the DATU2J routine (Figure 24.2). Then use DATCVT to convert from Julian back to year-month-day.

FIGURE 24.2
DATU2J Convert Date from Universal to Julian Format Function

```
... 1 ...+... 2 ...+... 3 ...+... 4 ...+... 5 ...+... 6 ...+... 7 ...+... 8
*-------------------------------------------------------------------
* DATU2J   Convert date from Universal to Julian format function
*
* Function:
*   Convert a date from Universal format to Julian format. The
*   Universal format is the number of days since 1st Jan 1900.
*   Use the Convert Date function DATCVT to convert the output
*   date from Julian format if required.
*
* Requires copy modules:
*   DATDS    -   Data structure for Date functions
*   STDCONST - Standard named constants
*
* Expects:
*   DTDATI - date_in_date in Universal format
*
* Returns:
*   DTVARO - date_out_var:
*     DTCNTO - date_out_cent
*     DTJULO - date_out_julian
*   DTERR  - date_err on error
*
* Example:
*   Convert the current Universal date in CURUDT into Julian
*   format and store the result in CURCNT and CURJUL.
*
C*                 MOVE CURUDT    DTDATI
C*                 EXSR DATU2J
C*                 MOVE DTCNTO    CURCNT
C*                 MOVE DTJULO    CURJUL
*
*-------------------------------------------------------------------
C         DATU2J    BEGSR
*
C                   MOVE *OFF     DTERR    1
C                   MOVE @DTPOS   @DTPOS   30
C                   MOVE @DTUNV   @DTUNV   60
C                   MOVE @DTCYR   @DTCYR   30
C                   MOVE @DTDAY   @DTDAY   30
*
C         DGTC      CHECKDTDATI   @DTPOS
*
* If no errors, convert to century/year and day in year, then
* concatenate into Julian format
*
C                   SELEC
*
C         @DTPOS    WHNE 0
C                   MOVE *ON      DTERR
*
C                   OTHER
C                   MOVE DTDATI   @DTUNV
C         @DTUNV    DIV  365.25   @DTCYR
C                   MVR            @DTDAY
C         @DTCYR    IFGT 0
C                   ADD  1        @DTDAY
C                   ENDIF
C                   MOVE @DTDAY   DTJULO
```

continued

FIGURE **24.2** *CONTINUED*

```
... 1 ...+... 2 ...+... 3 ...+... 4 ...+... 5 ...+... 6 ...+... 7 ...+... 8
C                      MOVEL@DTCYR    DTVARO
 *
C                      ENDSL
 *
C                      ENDSR
```

It took us a while to get the code for DATJ2U and DATU2J right. A quick
glance at the Figures 24.1 and 24.2 shows that they rely on multiplication and
division by 365.25 to round the result correctly. Obviously, this type of coding
needs thorough testing—random testing is not sufficient. So we wrote a program to test the algorithms with every date from January 1, 1900, to December
31, 2099. Remember when you write similar programs to test them thoroughly.
It's far easier to test programs during development than to try to debug them
once they are in production.

Let's now look at the date arithmetic programs to see how the routines are
used. Program ZDATADD (Figure 24.3) adds days to a date.

FIGURE **24.3**
ZDATADD Add Days to Date

```
... 1 ...+... 2 ...+... 3 ...+... 4 ...+... 5 ...+... 6 ...+... 7 ...+... 8
*------------------------------------------------------------------------
* ZDATADD    Add days to date
*
* Function:
*   Adds a number of days to a date in YMD format. The number
*   of days may be either positive or negative.
*
* Parameters:
*   INCNT  - in_cent
*   INDAT  - in_date
*   INDAY  - in_days
*   OUTCNT - out_cent
*   OUTDAT - out_date
*   ERRDS  - err_API_DS on error
*
* Example:
*   Add 7 days to the current date in CURDAT, of century
*   CURCNT.
*
C*                     MOVE CURCNT    INCNT
C*                     MOVE CURDAT    INDAT
C*                     Z-ADD7         INDAY
 *
C*                     CALL 'ZDATADD'
C*                     PARM           INCNT     10
C*                     PARM           INDAT     60
C*                     PARM           INDAY     50
C*                     PARM           OUTCNT    10
C*                     PARM           OUTDAT    60
C*                     PARM           ERRDS
 *
C*           ERRDLN    IFEQ 0
```

continued

FIGURE 24.3 *CONTINUED*

```
... 1 ...+... 2 ...+... 3 ...+... 4 ...+... 5 ...+... 6 ...+... 7 ...+... 8
C*                    MOVE OUTCNT    CURCNT
C*                    MOVE OUTDAT    CURDAT
C*                    ELSE
 *                    ...
C*                    ENDIF
 *
 *-----------------------------------------------------------------
 *
 *-----------------------------------------------------------------
 * Copy input modules
 *-----------------------------------------------------------------
/COPY DATDS
/COPY ERRDS
/COPY PGMSDS
/COPY RERDS
/COPY STDCONST
 *
 *-----------------------------------------------------------------
 * Entry point
 *-----------------------------------------------------------------
C          *ENTRY    PLIST
C                    PARM            INCNT  10
C                    PARM            INDAT  60
C                    PARM            INDAY  50
C                    PARM            OUTCNT 10
C                    PARM            OUTDAT 60
C                    PARM            RERDS
 *
 *-----------------------------------------------------------------
 * Mainline
 *-----------------------------------------------------------------
 *
 * Check for required number of parameters
 *
C          PSPRMS    IFLT 5
C                    MOVE *ON        *INLR
C                    RETRN
C                    ENDIF
 *
 * Initialize variables
 *
C                    RESETERRDS
C                    Z-ADD6          ERRPRM
C                    Z-ADD0          OUTCNT
C                    Z-ADD0          OUTDAT
C                    Z-ADD0          WKUNV  60
 *
 * Convert from YMD to Julian to Universal
 *
C                    MOVE INCNT      DTCNTI
C                    MOVE INDAT      DTDATI
C                    MOVE DTFYMD     DTFMTI
C                    MOVE DTFJUL     DTFMTO
C                    EXSR DATCVT
 *
C          DTERR     IFEQ *OFF
C                    MOVE DTVARO     DTVARI
C                    EXSR DATJ2U
C                    MOVELDTDATO     WKUNV
C                    ENDIF
```

continued

FIGURE **24.3** *CONTINUED*

```
... 1 ...+... 2 ...+... 3 ...+... 4 ...+... 5 ...+... 6 ...+... 7 ...+... 8
 *
 * Add days to date
 *
C           DTERR     IFEQ *OFF
C                     ADD  INDAY     WKUNV
C                     ENDIF
 *
 * Convert from Universal to Julian to YMD
 *
C           DTERR     IFEQ *OFF
C                     MOVELWKUNV     DTDATI
C                     EXSR DATU2J
C                     ENDIF
 *
C           DTERR     IFEQ *OFF
C                     MOVE DTVARO    DTVARI
C                     MOVE DTFJUL    DTFMTI
C                     MOVE DTFYMD    DTFMTO
C                     EXSR DATCVT
C                     MOVE DTCNTO    OUTCNT
C                     MOVE DTDATO    OUTDAT
C                     ENDIF
 *
 * Set return error
 *
C                     EXSR RERSET
 *
C                     RETRN
 *
 *------------------------------------------------------------------
 * Copy calc modules
 *------------------------------------------------------------------
/COPY DATCVT
/COPY DATJ2U
/COPY DATU2J
/COPY RERSET
```

To subtract days from a date, you make the number of days negative. ZDATADD simply consists of a comment header section and a short mainline that uses /COPY routines we've already developed, such as DATJ2U and DAT2UJ. As you can see, the simplicity of the program allows you to focus on its primary function without getting bogged down in the details of the secondary /COPY routines.

Using ZDATADD is simple. To add the lead time for a product in LDTIM to a purchase order date in PORDAT, to find the scheduled receipt date in PRCDAT, you code

```
C                     MOVE PORCNT    INCNT
C                     MOVE PORDAT    INDAT
C                     Z-ADDLDTIM     INDAY
 *
C                     CALL 'ZDATADD'
C                     PARM           INCNT  10
C                     PARM           INDAT  60
C                     PARM           INDAY  50
C                     PARM           OUTCNT 10
```

```
C                   PARM         OUTDAT 6Ø
C                   PARM         ERRDS
 *
C         ERRDLN    IFEQ Ø
C                   MOVE OUTCNT  PRCCNT
C                   MOVE OUTDAT  PRCDAT
C                   ELSE
  :                 handle error here
C                   ENDIF
```

Just like the date routines in the last chapter, ZDATADD requires a century indicator for each date that is passed to it: PORCNT for PORDAT; PRCCNT for PRCDAT.

To find the difference between two dates, you call the ZDATDIF program (Figure 24.4).

FIGURE 24.4
ZDATDIF Difference Between Dates

```
... 1 ...+... 2 ...+... 3 ...+... 4 ...+... 5 ...+... 6 ...+... 7 ...+... 8
*----------------------------------------------------------
* ZDATDIF    Difference between dates
*
* Function:
*    Calculates the difference in days between two dates in YMD
*    format. If the first date is earlier than the second date,
*    the difference is positive. If the first date is later than
*    the second date, the difference is negative.
*
* Parameters:
*    INCNT1 - in_cent1
*    INDAT1 - in_date1
*    INCNT2 - in_cent2
*    INDAT2 - in_date2
*    OUTDIF - out_diff
*    ERRDS  - err_API_DS on error
*
* Example:
*    Calculate the difference between the current date in
*    CURDAT, of century CURCNT, and the last month end date
*    in CLODAT, of century CLOCNT, and store the result in
*    DIFDAY.
*
C*                  MOVE CLOCNT  INCNT1
C*                  MOVE CLODAT  INDAT1
C*                  MOVE CURCNT  INCNT2
C*                  MOVE CURDAT  INDAT2
 *
C*                  CALL 'ZDATDIF'
C*                  PARM         INCNT1 1Ø
C*                  PARM         INDAT1 6Ø
C*                  PARM         INCNT2 1Ø
C*                  PARM         INDAT2 6Ø
C*                  PARM         OUTDIF 5Ø
C*                  PARM         ERRDS
 *
```

continued

FIGURE 24.4 *CONTINUED*

```
... 1 ...+... 2 ...+... 3 ...+... 4 ...+... 5 ...+... 6 ...+... 7 ...+... 8
C*            ERRDLN    IFEQ 0
C*                      Z-ADDOUTDIF    DIFDAY
C*                      ELSE
 *                      ...
C*                      ENDIF
 *
 *------------------------------------------------------------------------
 *
 *------------------------------------------------------------------------
 * Copy input modules
 *------------------------------------------------------------------------
/COPY DATDS
/COPY ERRDS
/COPY PGMSDS
/COPY RERDS
/COPY STDCONST
 *
 *------------------------------------------------------------------------
 * Entry point
 *------------------------------------------------------------------------
C            *ENTRY    PLIST
C                      PARM           INCNT1 10
C                      PARM           INDAT1 60
C                      PARM           INCNT2 10
C                      PARM           INDAT2 60
C                      PARM           OUTDIF 50
C                      PARM           RERDS
 *
 *------------------------------------------------------------------------
 * Mainline
 *------------------------------------------------------------------------
 *
 * Check for required number of parameters
 *
C            PSPRMS    IFLT 5
C                      MOVE *ON       *INLR
C                      RETRN
C                      ENDIF
 *
 * Initialize variables
 *
C                      RESETERRDS
C                      Z-ADD6         ERRPRM
C                      Z-ADD0         OUTDIF
C                      Z-ADD0         WKUNV1 60
C                      Z-ADD0         WKUNV2 60
 *
 * Convert first date from YMD to Julian to Universal
 *
C                      MOVE INCNT1    DTCNTI
C                      MOVE INDAT1    DTDATI
C                      MOVE DTFYMD    DTFMTI
C                      MOVE DTFJUL    DTFMTO
C                      EXSR DATCVT
 *
C            DTERR     IFEQ *OFF
C                      MOVE DTVARO    DTVARI
C                      EXSR DATJ2U
C                      MOVELDTDATO    WKUNV1
C                      ENDIF
 *
```

continued

FIGURE 24.4 CONTINUED

```
... 1 ...+... 2 ...+... 3 ...+... 4 ...+... 5 ...+... 6 ...+... 7 ...+... 8
 * Convert second date from YMD to Julian to Universal
 *
C           DTERR     IFEQ *OFF
C                     MOVE INCNT2    DTCNTI
C                     MOVE INDAT2    DTDATI
C                     MOVE DTFYMD    DTFMTI
C                     MOVE DTFJUL    DTFMTO
C                     EXSR DATCVT
C                     ENDIF
 *
C           DTERR     IFEQ *OFF
C                     MOVE DTVARO    DTVARI
C                     EXSR DATJ2U
C                     MOVELDTDATO    WKUNV1
C                     ENDIF
 *
 * Calculate difference between dates
 *
C           DTERR     IFEQ *OFF
C           WKUNV2    SUB  WKUNV1    OUTDIF
C                     ENDIF
 *
 * Set return error
 *
C                     EXSR RERSET
 *
C                     RETRN
 *
 *-------------------------------------------------------------------------
 * Copy calc modules
 *-------------------------------------------------------------------------
/COPY DATCVT
/COPY DATJ2U
/COPY RERSET
```

For example, to calculate the number of days between the scheduled ship-ment date for an order in OSCDAT and the actual shipment date in OACDAT, and then store the result in DIFDAY, you code

```
C                     MOVE OSCCNT    INCNT1
C                     MOVE OSCDAT    INDAT1
C                     MOVE OACCNT    INCNT2
C                     MOVE OACDAT    INDAT2
 *
C                     CALL 'ZDATDIF'
C                     PARM           INCNT1 10
C                     PARM           INDAT1 60
C                     PARM           INCNT2 10
C                     PARM           INDAT2 60
C                     PARM           OUTDIF 50
C                     PARM           ERRDS
 *
C           ERRDLN    IFEQ 0
C                     Z-ADDOUTDIF    DIFDAY
C                     ELSE
    :                 handle error here
C                     ENDIF
```

If the actual date is later than the scheduled date, the result is positive. If the actual date is earlier than the scheduled date, the result is negative. If both dates are the same, the result is zero.

You can easily write your own date functions using the /COPY modules in this chapter and Chapter 23. For example, you might need a function that calculates the day of the week for any date. To do this, first find out the day of the week for our base date of January 1, 1900. Then convert any date to universal format and divide by 7; a result of 0 means the date was on the base day; for any other result, just count forward from the base day.

Chapter 25

Eponentiation in RPG

With this RPG program, you can code most complex business calculations that require exponentiation.

As a rule, RPG's simple arithmetic operations can handle most situations. But every rule has its exceptions — as you know if you've tried using RPG to calculate compound interest, or the annual percentage yield on an investment, as defined by the U.S. Truth in Savings Act (TISA). Such calculations use exponentiation; and, unfortunately, RPG/400 doesn't have an EXP opcode. However, this chapter provides the CLCEXP program (Figure 25.1) to perform the same function. CLCEXP is provided here as a called program. If you absolutely must, you could modify it to be a /COPY module for better performance. However, as coded, it performs well for almost all purposes.

FIGURE 25.1
CLCEXP RPG Program

```
... 1 ...+... 2 ...+... 3 ...+... 4 ...+... 5 ...+... 6 ...+... 7 ...+... 8
 *-----------------------------------------------------------------------
 * CLCEXP - Calculate exponent of number raised to power
 *
 * Function:
 *   Calculates the exponent of a number raised to any power.
 *   Note: the number must be positive.
 *
 * Parameters:
 *   CLNBR  - calc_number
 *   CLPWR  - calc_power
 *   CLEXP  - calc_number
 *   CLERR  - calc_error (*ON if calc_exponent is truncated)
 *
 * Example:
 *   Raise 2 to the power of 3.5 and place the answer in RESULT.
 *
C*               Z-ADD2       CLNBR
C*               Z-ADD3.5     CLPWR
 *
C*               CALL 'CLCEXP'
C*               PARM         CLNBR 156
C*               PARM         CLPWR 156
C*               PARM         CLEXP 156
C*               PARM         CLERR 1
 *
C*      CLERR    IFEQ *OFF
C*               Z-ADDCLEXP   RESULT
C*               ELSE
 *               ...
C*               ENDIF
 *
```

continued

FIGURE 25.1 *CONTINUED*

```
... 1 ...+... 2 ...+... 3 ...+... 4 ...+... 5 ...+... 6 ...+... 7 ...+... 8
 *-----------------------------------------------------------------------
 *
 *-----------------------------------------------------------------------
 * Named constants
 *-----------------------------------------------------------------------
I             -.69314718        C       LNHLF
I             0.69314718        C       LN2
I             2.30258509        C       LN10
I             6.90775527        C       LN1000
 *
 *-----------------------------------------------------------------------
 * Copy input modules
 *-----------------------------------------------------------------------
/COPY PGMSDS
 *
 *-----------------------------------------------------------------------
 * Entry point
 *-----------------------------------------------------------------------
C           *ENTRY    PLIST
C                     PARM           CLNBR  156
C                     PARM           CLPWR  156
C                     PARM           CLEXP  156
C                     PARM           CLERR  1
 *
 *-----------------------------------------------------------------------
 * Mainline
 *-----------------------------------------------------------------------
 *
 * Check for required number of parameters
 *
C           PSPRMS    IFLT 4
C                     MOVE *ON        *INLR
C                     RETRN
C                     ENDIF
 *
C                     Z-ADD0          CLEXP
C                     MOVE *OFF        CLERR
 *
 * Check for power equal to 0
 *
C           CLPWR     IFEQ 0
C                     Z-ADD1          CLEXP
C                     RETRN
C                     ENDIF
 *
 * Check for number equal to 0 or 1
 *
C           CLNBR     IFEQ 0
C           CLNBR     OREQ 1
C                     Z-ADDCLNBR      CLEXP
C                     RETRN
C                     ENDIF
 *
 * result = exp( ln( number ) * power )
 *
C           CLNBR     IFGT 0
C                     Z-ADDCLNBR      NUM
C                     ELSE
C                     Z-SUBCLNBR      NUM
C                     ENDIF
 *
```

continued

FIGURE 25.1 CONTINUED

```
... 1 ...+... 2 ...+... 3 ...+... 4 ...+... 5 ...+... 6 ...+... 7 ...+... 8
C                      EXSR CLCLN
 *
C           MTHERR     IFEQ *OFF
 *
C                      MULT CLPWR     LN
C                      EXSR CLCEXP
C           CLNBR      IFGT 0
C                      Z-ADDEXP       CLEXP
C                      ELSE
C                      Z-SUBEXP       CLEXP
C                      ENDIF
 *
C                      ENDIF
 *
C                      MOVE MTHERR    CLERR
 *
C                      RETRN
 *
 *------------------------------------------------------------------------
 * CLCLN  - Calculates natural logarithm of number
 *
 * The natural logarithm of a number can be expressed by the
 * power series:
 *   ln x = (x-1) - ((x-1)**2)/2 + ((x-1)**3)/3 - ...
 *                                       (for 0 < x <= 2)
 *------------------------------------------------------------------------
C           CLCLN      BEGSR
 *
 * Declare global variables
 *
C                      Z-ADDLN        LN     159
C                      Z-ADDNUM       NUM    156
C                      MOVE *OFF      MTHERR  1
 *
 * Declare local variables
 *
C                      Z-ADD1         @INCR  159
C                      Z-ADD0         @EXP2  159
C                      Z-ADD0         @INT    70
C                      Z-ADD0         @MANT  159
C                      Z-ADD-1        @PWRN  159
C                      Z-ADD0         @SUMM  159
 *
 * Number must be greater than 0
 *
C           NUM        IFLE 0
C                      MOVE *ON       MTHERR
C                      GOTO ENDLN
C                      ENDIF
 *
 * Convert number to mantissa and exponent in the range
 * (1 <= mantissa <= 1.34) to satisfy the limits of the
 * summation and improve performance.
 *
C           NUM        IFLT 1000000
C                      Z-ADDNUM       @MANT
C                      ELSE
C                      MOVE NUM       @MANT
C                      Z-ADDLN1000    @EXP2
C                      ENDIF
```

continued

FIGURE 25.1 *CONTINUED*

```
... 1 ...+... 2 ...+... 3 ...+... 4 ...+... 5 ...+... 6 ...+... 7 ...+... 8
 *
C           @MANT       DOWLT1
C                       MULT 10      @MANT
C                       SUB  LN10    @EXP2
C                       ENDDO
 *
C           @MANT       DOWGE10
C                       MULT 0.1     @MANT
C                       ADD  LN10    @EXP2
C                       ENDDO
 *
C           @MANT       DOWGE1.34
C                       MULT 0.5     @MANT
C                       ADD  LN2     @EXP2
C                       ENDDO
 *
 * Summate power series while increment is not 0
 *
C                       SUB  1       @MANT
 *
C           @INCR       DOWNE0
 *
C                       MULT @MANT   @PWRN
C                       Z-SUB@PWRN   @PWRN
C                       ADD  1       @INT
C           @PWRN       DIV  @INT    @INCR
C                       ADD  @INCR   @SUMM
 *
C                       ENDDO
 *
C           @SUMM       ADD  @EXP2   LN        H
 *
C           ENDLN       ENDSR
 *
 *-----------------------------------------------------------------------------
 * CLCEXP - Calculates exponential of a natural logarithm
 *
 * The exponential of a natural logarithm can be expressed by
 * the power series:
 *   exp x = 1 + x + (x**2)/2! + (x**3)/3! + ...
 *         = 1 + x + (x)*(x/2) + (x)*(x/2)*(x/3) + ...
 *                                              (for all x)
 *-----------------------------------------------------------------------------
C           CLCEXP      BEGSR
 *
 * Declare global variables
 *
C                       Z-ADDEXP     EXP      156
C                       Z-ADDLN      LN       159
C                       MOVE *OFF    MTHERR   1
 *
 * Declare local variables
 *
C                       Z-ADD1       @INCR    159
C                       Z-ADD1       @EXP     156
C                       Z-ADD0       @INT      70
C                       Z-ADD0       @INTMX   150
C                       Z-ADD0       @MANT    159
C                       Z-ADD1       @SUMM    159
 *
```

continued

FIGURE 25.1 *CONTINUED*

```
... 1 ...+... 2 ...+... 3 ...+... 4 ...+... 5 ...+... 6 ...+... 7 ...+... 8
 * Convert number to mantissa and exponent in the range
 * (ln .5 <= mantissa <= 1) to increase the accuracy and
 * the performance of the summation.
 *
C                       Z-ADDLN      @MANT
 *
C           @MANT       DOWLTLNHLF
C                       ADD  LN10    @MANT
C                       MULT 0.1     @EXP
C                       ENDDO
 *
C           @MANT       DOWGT0
C                       SUB  LN10    @MANT
C                       MULT 10      @EXP
C                       ENDDO
 *
C           @MANT       DOWLTLNHLF
C                       ADD  LN2     @MANT
C                       MULT 0.5     @EXP
C                       ENDDO
 *
 * Summate power series while increment is not 0
 *
C           @INCR       DOWNE0
 *
C                       ADD  1       @INT
C                       MULT @MANT   @INCR
C                       DIV  @INT    @INCR
C                       ADD  @INCR   @SUMM
 *
C                       ENDDO
 *
C           @SUMM       MULT @EXP    EXP        H
 *
 * Check for integer truncation
 *
C           @SUMM       MULT @EXP    @INTMX
 *
C           EXP         IFLT @INTMX
C           @EXP        OREQ 0
C                       MOVE @ON     MTHERR
C                       END
 *
C                       ENDSR
```

CLCEXP lets you quickly perform exponentiation in RPG, accurate to seven significant digits. You call CLCEXP with four parameters:

CLNBR	declares the number to be raised to a power
CLPWR	declares the power applied to CLNBR
CLEXP	declares the result returned by program CLCEXP
CLERR	declares a logical variable used to return errors from the program; CLERR will be set on if integer truncation occurs

You must declare the first three parameters as numeric variables of 15 digits with six decimal places. You declare the last parameter as a character variable of 1 byte.

Let's see how to use CLCEXP to calculate the annual percentage yield on savings, which is defined by the U.S. TISA as

Yield = (1+(Interest/Principal))**(365/Days)-1

The following code snippet shows how to implement the yield formula in RPG:

```
C            INTRST    DIV  PRINC    CLNBR
C                      ADD  1        CLNBR
 *
C            365       DIV  DAYS     CLPWR
 *
C                      CALL 'CLCEXP'
C                      PARM          CLNBR  156
C                      PARM          CLPWR  156
C                      PARM          CLEXP  156
C                      PARM          CLERR    1
 *
C            CLERR     IFEQ *OFF
C            CLEXP     SUB  1        YIELD
C                      ELSE
C                      Z-ADD0        YIELD
C                      ENDIF
```

The yield formula is broken down into four simple steps. First, calculate parameter CLNBR (the number to raise to a power), as shown in the first two lines of code. Second, calculate parameter CLPWR (the power to raise the number), as shown in the third line. Third, call CLCEXP to raise the number in CLNBR to the power in CLPWR, as shown in the next several lines of code. And last, subtract 1 from the exponent returned by CLCEXP to get the annual percentage yield. Notice that, as always with RPG, you code the calculation from the innermost set of parentheses outward.

Program CLCEXP has one limitation you need to keep in mind. Because of the limited size of numeric fields in RPG, the result returned by CLCEXP is accurate only to about seven significant digits. Although this degree of accuracy is fine for most purposes, it could pose problems with some formulae in financial applications. To determine whether or not CLCEXP is accurate enough for your requirements, you should first check any calculation you want to use with it. For example, let's look at the formula for annual yield shown above. Interest of $136.99 for 100 days on a principal of $10,000 produces a yield of 0.050916, which is correct when rounded to four decimal places. Substituting 1 day or 365 days into the calculation produces results with the same degree of accuracy, so CLCEXP is fine for this sort of calculation.

However, CLCEXP may not be suitable for some other calculations. For example, the amount due on a loan subject to compound interest can be defined as

AmountDue = LoanAmount*((1+InterestRate)**Periods)

Let's look at the right side of the calculation, which produces the compound interest rate. Using CLCEXP, a rate of 20 percent over 25½ years produces a compound rate of 104.501315; the correct result, however, is 104.5014. The difference may not seem like much, but it would result in a rounding down of the amount due of 1 cent per 100 dollars of the loan amount.

CLCEXP is a powerful RPG ally for complex statistical applications, with acceptable performance and accuracy for most jobs. Remember, though, to test CLCEXP with your financial algorithms to ensure that its RPG-constrained accuracy is acceptable.

Chapter 26

Using User Spaces

Use these modules to simplify working with user spaces in your programs.

A user space is an object used to store temporary data required by a program. User spaces are not organized by records and fields; rather, they are a contiguous stream of bytes with no implicit organization. A user space's storage organization is a bit like that of a data area; however, where a data area can be a maximum of 2,000 bytes, a user space can be up to a whoppin' 16 MB.

IBM list APIs, such as the List Objects API (QUSLOBJ), direct their output to a user space that you can process in an RPG program. User spaces also provide a fast and efficient means for storing large amounts of application data required by your programs. In this chapter, we cover the four basic steps you need to understand for working with user spaces: create, change, retrieve, and delete. In the next chapter, we look at how to retrieve the information generated by IBM list APIs.

The /COPY modules included in this chapter are

USDS	provides the USDS user space data structures required by the following members (Figure 26.1)
USCRT	creates a user space (Figure 26.2)
USCHG	changes the contents of a user space (Figure 26.3)
USRTV	retrieves the contents of a user space (Figure 26.4)
USDLT	deletes a user space (Figure 26.5)

You will also need the ERRDS module shown in Figure 2.2 (Chapter 2).

To use the modules, you include the ERRDS and USDS (Figure 26.1) data structures at the end of the I-specs.

FIGURE 26.1

USDS User Space Data Structure

```
... 1 ...+... 2 ...+... 3 ...+... 4 ...+... 5 ...+... 6 ...+... 7 ...+... 8
*-----------------------------------------------------------------
* USDS - Data structures for User Space functions
*
* Function:
*   Defines data structures for User Space functions.
*
* USDS   - user_space_DS:
*   USQNAM - user_space_qual_name
*     USNAM  - user_space_name
```

continued

FIGURE 26.1 *CONTINUED*

```
... 1 ...+... 2 ...+... 3 ...+... 4 ...+... 5 ...+... 6 ...+... 7 ...+... 8
*     USLIB  - user_space_lib
*     USATR  - user_space_attr
*     USSIZ  - user_space_initial_size
*     USVAL  - user_space_initial_value
*     USAUT  - user_space_authority
*     USTXT  - user_space_text_desc
*     USRPL  - user_space_replace
*     USPTR  - user_space_data_ptr
*     USLEN  - user_space_data_len
*     USDTA  - user_space_data
*-------------------------------------------------------------------
IUSDS       IDS
I                                         1  20 USQNAM
I                                         1  10 USNAM
I                                        11  20 USLIB
*
I                                        21  30 USATR
I                                    B   31  340USSIZ
I                                        35  35 USVAL
I I         '*CHANGE'                    36  45 USAUT
I                                        46  95 USTXT
I I         '*YES'                       96 105 USRPL
*
I                                    B  106 1090USPTR
I                                    B  110 1130USLEN
*
*-------------------------------------------------------------------
* UDDS   - user_space_data_DS
*-------------------------------------------------------------------
IUDDS       IDS                            9999
```

The remaining four modules include subroutines for performing user space functions, and they should be included at the end of the C-specs. We normally stick to the convention of coding a single subroutine in each C-spec copy module, and of using the same name for both the subroutine and the module. So the USCRT member contains subroutine USCRT, USCHG contains subroutine USCHG, and so on. Each subroutine uses the ERRDS data structure to provide feedback about runtime errors. After executing each of the subroutines provided, to test for errors you must check the ERRDLN field (which is returned in the ERRDS data structure after each call to a user-space API).

```
C           ERRDLN    IFNE 0
    :                 handle error here
C                     ENDIF
```

To create a user space, you use the USCRT (Figure 26.2) subroutine, specifying the name and library of the user space and its size.

FIGURE 26.2
USCRT Create User Space Function

```
... 1 ...+... 2 ...+... 3 ...+... 4 ...+... 5 ...+... 6 ...+... 7 ...+... 8
*-------------------------------------------------------------------------
* USCRT - Create User Space function
*
* Function:
*   Create a user space. Note: only IBM list APIs can extend
*   the size of a user space, so take care in specifying the
*   size of all other user spaces.
*
* Requires copy modules:
*   USDS   - Data structures for User Space functions
*
* Expects:
*   USQNAM - user_space_qual_name:
*     USNAM  - user_space_name
*     USLIB  - user_space_lib
*   USSIZ  - user_space_initial_size
*
* Returns:
*   USQNAM - user_space_qual_name
*   ERRDS  - err_API_DS
*
* Example:
*   Create a user space called MYSPC in MYLIB with a size
*   of 8000 bytes, and save the qualified name in MYUS.
*
C*                     MOVEL'MYSPC'  USNAM     P
C*                     MOVEL'MYLIB'  USLIB     P
C*                     Z-ADD8000     USSIZ
C*                     EXSR USCRT
*
C*          ERRDLN     IFNE 0
C*                     MOVELUSQNAM   MYUS
C*                     ELSE
*                      ...
C*                     ENDIF
*
*-------------------------------------------------------------------------
C           USCRT      BEGSR
*
C                      CALL 'QUSCRTUS'
C                      PARM          USQNAM
C                      PARM          USATR
C                      PARM          USSIZ
C                      PARM          USVAL
C                      PARM          USAUT
C                      PARM          USTXT
C                      PARM          USRPL
C                      PARM          ERRDS
*
C                      ENDSR
```

To create a user space of 8,000 bytes called INVUS in library QTEMP, you code

```
C                      MOVEL'INVUS'  USNAM     P
C                      MOVEL'QTEMP'  USLIB     P
C                      Z-ADD8000     USSIZ
C                      EXSR USCRT
C           ERRDLN     IFNE 0
```

```
                 :                      handle error here
     C                                  ENDIF
```

Once you have created a user space, you can change or retrieve its contents as often as you want. To change the contents of a user space, you use the USCHG subroutine (Figure 26.3), specifying a pointer to the starting position you want to change, the length of the data, and the data itself.

FIGURE 26.3
USCHG Change User Space Function

```
... 1 ...+... 2 ...+... 3 ...+... 4 ...+... 5 ...+... 6 ...+... 7 ...+... 8
*--------------------------------------------------------------------------
* USCHG - Change User Space function
*
* Function:
*   Changes the contents of part of an existing user space.
*
* Requires copy modules:
*   USDS   - Data structures for User Space functions
*
* Expects:
*   USQNAM - user_space_qual_name:
*     USNAM  - user_space_name
*     USLIB  - user_space_lib
*   USPTR  - user_space_data_ptr
*   USLEN  - user_space_data_len
*   UDDS   - user_space_data_DS
*
* Returns:
*   ERRDS  - err_API_DS
*
* Example:
*   Replace the first 80 characters of a user space called
*   MYSPC in library MYLIB with the contents of the field DATA.
*
C*                      MOVEL'MYSPC'    USNAM     P
C*                      MOVEL'MYLIB'    USLIB     P
C*                      Z-ADD1          USPTR
C*                      Z-ADD80         USLEN
C*                      MOVELDATA       UDDS      P
C*                      EXSR USCHG
*
C*        ERRDLN        IFNE 0
*                       ...
C*                      ENDIF
*
*--------------------------------------------------------------------------
C         USCHG         BEGSR
*
C                       CALL 'QUSCHGUS'
C                       PARM            USQNAM
C                       PARM            USPTR
C                       PARM            USLEN
C                       PARM            UDDS
* Note: The following line specifies a zero, not the letter O.
C                       PARM '0'        US@CHG    1
C                       PARM            ERRDS
*
C                       ENDSR
```

To store the contents of an INVDS data structure of 80 bytes, starting in position 1 of the INVUS user space, you code

```
C                         MOVEL'INVUS'   USNAM     P
C                         MOVEL'QTEMP'   USLIB     P
C                         Z-ADD1         USPTR
C                         Z-ADD80        USLEN
C                         MOVELINVDS     UDDS      P
C                         EXSR USCHG
C            ERRDLN       IFNE 0
   :                      handle error here
C                         ENDIF
```

You use the USRTV subroutine (Figure 26.4) to retrieve the contents of a user space.

FIGURE 26.4
USRTV Retrieve User Space Function

```
... 1 ...+... 2 ...+... 3 ...+... 4 ...+... 5 ...+... 6 ...+... 7 ...+... 8
 *-----------------------------------------------------------------
 * USRTV - Retrieve User Space function
 *
 * Function:
 *   Retrieves the contents of part of an existing user space.
 *
 * Requires copy modules:
 *   USDS   - Data structures for User Space functions
 *
 * Expects:
 *   USQNAM - user_space_qual_name:
 *     USNAM  - user_space_name
 *     USLIB  - user_space_lib
 *   USPTR  - user_space_data_ptr
 *   USLEN  - user_space_data_len
 *
 * Returns:
 *   UDDS   - user_space_data_DS
 *   ERRDS  - err_API_DS
 *
 * Example:
 *   Retrieve the first 80 characters of a user space called
 *   MYSPC in library MYLIB into the field DATA.
 *
C*                        MOVEL'MYSPC'   USNAM     P
C*                        MOVEL'MYLIB'   USLIB     P
C*                        Z-ADD1         USPTR
C*                        Z-ADD80        USLEN
C*                        EXSR USRTV
 *
C*           ERRDLN       IFEQ 0
C*                        MOVELUDDS      DATA      P
C*                        ELSE
 *                        ...
C*                        ENDIF
 *
 *-----------------------------------------------------------------
C            USRTV        BEGSR
 *
C                         CALL 'QUSRTVUS'
```

continued

FIGURE 26.4 *CONTINUED*

```
... 1 ...+... 2 ...+... 3 ...+... 4 ...+... 5 ...+... 6 ...+... 7 ...+... 8
C                      PARM           USQNAM
C                      PARM           USPTR
C                      PARM           USLEN
C                      PARM           UDDS
C                      PARM           ERRDS
 *
C                      ENDSR
```

Just as with USCHG, USRTV needs to know the position and length of the data, and it requires a variable to store the data returned from the user space:

```
C                      MOVEL'INVUS'   USNAM   P
C                      MOVEL'QTEMP'   USLIB   P
C                      Z-ADD1         USPTR
C                      Z-ADD80        USLEN
C                      EXSR USRTV
C         ERRDLN       IFNE 0
   :                   handle error here
C                      ELSE
C                      MOVELIUDDS     INVDS   P
C                      ENDIF
```

Finally, to delete a user space, you use the USDLT subroutine (Figure 26.5).

FIGURE 26.5
USDLT Delete User Space Function

```
... 1 ...+... 2 ...+... 3 ...+... 4 ...+... 5 ...+... 6 ...+... 7 ...+... 8
*---------------------------------------------------------------------------
* USDLT - Delete User Space function
*
* Function:
*   Deletes an existing user space.
*
* Requires copy modules:
*   USDS   - Data structures for User Space functions
*
* Expects:
*   USQNAM - user_space_qual_name:
*     USNAM - user_space_name
*     USLIB - user_space_lib
*
* Returns:
*   ERRDS  - err_API_DS
*
* Example:
*   Delete a user space called MYSPC in MYLIB.
*
C*                     MOVEL'MYSPC'   USNAM   P
C*                     MOVEL'MYLIB'   USLIB   P
C*                     EXSR USDLT
 *
C*        ERRDLN       IFNE 0
 *                     ...
C*                     ENDIF
 *
```

continued

FIGURE 26.5 CONTINUED

```
... 1 ...+... 2 ...+... 3 ...+... 4 ...+... 5 ...+... 6 ...+... 7 ...+... 8
*----------------------------------------------------------------------
C         USDLT     BEGSR
 *
C                   CALL 'QUSDLTUS'
C                   PARM            USQNAM
C                   PARM            ERRDS
 *
C                   ENDSR
```

You need to specify the name and library of the user space:

```
C                          MOVEL'INVUS'   USNAM   P
C                          MOVEL'QTEMP'   USLIB   P
C                          EXSR USDLT
C          ERRDLN          IFNE 0
   :                       handle error here
C                          ENDIF
```

The copy modules simplify the code required to work with user spaces, but how and when should you use them? As we said earlier, user spaces are ideal for storing large amounts of application data required by a program. For example, consider a job that posts a batch of inventory transactions. Each transaction could contain many detail lines. The job may have to validate each transaction and reject any transaction that has any line in error. This type of processing requires two passes of the data fl one for error checking, and one for posting. Instead of performing two sets of random I/O on the data, or using work files, you can store a complete transaction in a user space and then retrieve it once for each pass.

Also note that user spaces can be shared among programs, so you can store the data in one program and then pass the name of the user space, together with its current size, to separate subprograms for validity checking and posting. This capability improves the modularity of your code with very little impact on performance.

Chapter 27

Using List APIs

Use these modules for easy access to the information returned by OS/400 list APIs.

The OS/400-provided list APIs are powerful tools for retrieving information about various types of objects on the AS/400. You can use the APIs to write programming tools that display or perform actions on lists of objects. Each list API outputs information to a user space in a common format to simplify the retrieval of entries from the list. A user space created by a list API contains a number of sections, the most important of which are a generic header that includes pointers to the list data, and the actual list entries. These sections of information are unique to each API and are documented in the *System API Reference* (SC41-3801).

In this chapter, we provide routines to access the entries returned by any list API, using the List Object API (QUSLOBJ) as an example. The /COPY modules included in this chapter are

OBJLDS	includes data structures required to list objects (Figure 27.1)
ULDS	includes data structures required to retrieve the list entries in a user space (Figure 27.2)
OBJLST	lists objects (Figure 27.3)
ULHRTV	retrieves the list header from a user space (Figure 27.4)
ULERTV	retrieves a list entry from a user space (Figure 27.5)

FIGURE 27.1
OBJLDS Object List Data Structure

```
... 1 ...+... 2 ...+... 3 ...+... 4 ...+... 5 ...+... 6 ...+... 7 ...+... 8
*-----------------------------------------------------------------------
* OBJLDS - Data structure for Object List function
*
* Function:
*   Defines the data structure for the entries created by the
*   List Object function, OBJLST. Supports format 1 (basic data)
*   and format 2 (descriptive data).
*
* OBJDS - obj_list_DS:
*   Format 1:
*     OLOBJ  - obj_list_obj
*     OLLIB  - obj_list_lib
*     OLTYP  - obj_list_obj_type
*   Format 2:
*     OLSTS  - obj_list_status
*     OLATR  - obj_list_attr
```

continued

FIGURE 27.1 *CONTINUED*

```
... 1 ...+... 2 ...+... 3 ...+... 4 ...+... 5 ...+... 6 ...+... 7 ...+... 8
 *      OLTXT  - obj_list_text_desc
 *      OLUATR - obj_list_user_attr
 *      OL102  - obj_list_filler_102
 *-------------------------------------------------------------------------
IOBJDS      IDS
I                                            1  10 OLOBJ
I                                           11  20 OLLIB
I                                           21  30 OLTYP
 *
I                                           31  31 OLSTS
I                                           32  41 OLATR
I                                           42  91 OLTXT
I                                           92 101 OLUATR
I                                          102 108 OL102
 *
 *-------------------------------------------------------------------------
 *      OL1FMT - obj_list1_fmt
 *      OL2FMT - obj_list2_fmt
 *-------------------------------------------------------------------------
I              'OBJL0100'              C         OL1FMT
I              'OBJL0200'              C         OL2FMT
```

FIGURE 27.2

ULDS User Space List Data Structure

```
... 1 ...+... 2 ...+... 3 ...+... 4 ...+... 5 ...+... 6 ...+... 7 ...+... 8
 *-------------------------------------------------------------------------
 * ULDS - Data structure for User Space List functions
 *
 * Function:
 *   Defines the data structure for the list header information
 *   in a user space created by an IBM compatible List API.
 *   Use the ULHRTV function to retrieve the data structure.
 *
 * ULDS    - user_space_list_header_DS:
 *   ULARA  - user_space_user_area
 *   ULGSIZ - user_space_generic_header_size
 *   ULRLS  - user_space_release_level
 *   ULFMT  - user_space_API_format
 *   ULAPI  - user_space_API_name
 *   ULDTM  - user_space_data_time_stamp
 *   ULSTS  - user_space_status (Complete, Incomplete, Partial)
 *   ULSIZ  - user_space_size
 *   ULPOFF - user_space_parm_offset
 *   ULPSIZ - user_space_parm_size
 *   ULHOFF - user_space_header_offset
 *   ULHSIZ - user_space_header_size
 *   ULLOFF - user_space_list_offset
 *   ULLSIZ - user_space_list_size
 *   ULEOCR - user_space_entry_occurs
 *   ULESIZ - user_space_entry_size
 *-------------------------------------------------------------------------
IULDS       IDS
I                                            1  64 ULARA
I                                         B 65 680ULGSIZ
I                                           69  72 ULRLS
I                                           73  80 ULFMT
```

continued

FIGURE 27.2 *CONTINUED*

```
... 1 ...+... 2 ...+... 3 ...+... 4 ...+... 5 ...+... 6 ...+... 7 ...+... 8
I                                        81   90 ULAPI
I                                        91  103 ULDTM
I                                       104  104 ULSTS
I                                     B 105 1080ULSIZ
I                                     B 109 1120ULPOFF
I                                     B 113 1160ULPSIZ
I                                     B 117 1200ULHOFF
I                                     B 121 1240ULHSIZ
I                                     B 125 1280ULLOFF
I                                     B 129 1320ULLSIZ
I                                     B 133 1360ULEOCR
I                                     B 137 1400ULESIZ
 *
 *-----------------------------------------------------------------
 *    ULHPTR - user_space_header_ptr
 *    ULHLEN - user_space_header_len
 *-----------------------------------------------------------------
I              1                      C         ULHPTR
I            140                      C         ULHLEN
```

You will also need the modules described in Chapter 26 to create and delete user spaces.

Although we refer to many copy modules in this chapter, very little specific code is required to use them. In addition to what you learned about user spaces in Chapter 26, you need only four short sections of code to process an object list. First, you code the copy statements for the required modules, putting these four copy statements at the end of your RPG program's I-specs:

```
/COPY ERRDS
/COPY OBJLDS
/COPY ULDS
/COPY USDS
```

and putting the following five copy statements at the end of your RPG program's C-specs:

```
/COPY OBJLST
/COPY ULERTV
/COPY ULHRTV
/COPY USCRT
/COPY USDLT
```

Then, to use the QUSLOBJ API, you create a user space and use the OBJLST subroutine (Figure 27.3), which writes a list of objects to the user space.

FIGURE 27.3

OBJLST Object List Function

```
... 1 ...+... 2 ...+... 3 ...+... 4 ...+... 5 ...+... 6 ...+... 7 ...+... 8
*-----------------------------------------------------------------------
* OBJLST - List objects function
*
* Function:
*   Creates a list of objects of a type in a library. The list
*   is stored in a user space. Use the USCRT function to create
*   the user space. Use the ULHRTV function to retrieve the
*   list header, and the ULERTV function to retrieve the list
*   entries.
*
* Requires copy modules:
*   OBJLDS - Data structure for Object List function
*   USDS   - Data structures for User Space functions
*   ULDS   - Data structure for User Space List functions
*
* Expects:
*   USQNAM - user_space_qual_name:
*     USNAM  - user_space_name
*     USLIB  - user_space_lib
*   ULFMT  - user_space_API_format of:
*     OL1FMT - obj_list1_fmt
*     OL2FMT - obj_list2_fmt
*   OLOBJ  - obj_list_obj or generic object or *ALL
*   OLLIB  - obj_list_lib or *ALL or *ALLUSR or *CURLIB
*                          or *LIBL or *USRLIBL
*   OLTYP  - obj_list_type
*
* Returns:
*   ERRDS  - err_API_DS
*
* Example:
*   Output a list of objects with the generic name INV* of
*   type *FILE in library APPLIB to the user space MYSPC
*   in library MYLIB. The list contains the format 2
*   information OL2FMT for each object.
*
C*                  MOVEL'MYSPC'    USNAM       P
C*                  MOVEL'MYLIB'    USLIB       P
C*                  MOVE OL2FMT     ULFMT
C*                  MOVEL'APPLIB'   OLLIB       P
C*                  MOVEL'INV*'     OLOBJ       P
C*                  MOVEL'*FILE'    OLTYP       P
C*                  EXSR OBJLST
*

*-----------------------------------------------------------------------
C         OBJLST    BEGSR
*
C                   MOVELOLOBJ      OL@QNM
C                   MOVE OLLIB      OL@QNM
C                   MOVE OLTYP      OL@TYP
*
C                   CALL 'QUSLOBJ'
C                   PARM            USQNAM
C                   PARM            ULFMT
C                   PARM            OL@QNM 20
C                   PARM            OL@TYP 10
C                   PARM            ERRDS
*
C                   ENDSR
```

To output a detailed list of all inventory files in library APPLIB to a user space called OBJUS in QTEMP, you code

```
 * Create a 50,000 byte user space
C                           MOVEL'OBJUS'    USNAM     P
C                           MOVEL'QTEMP'    USLIB     P
C                           Z-ADD500000     USSIZ
C                           EXSR USCRT
  *
 * Call the QUSLOBJ API to list all the *FILE
 * objects in the APPLIB with names that start
 * with INV.
C                           MOVEL'OBJUS'    USNAM     P
C                           MOVEL'QTEMP'    USLIB     P
C                           MOVE OL2FMT     ULFMT
C                           MOVEL'APPLIB'   OLLIB     P
C                           MOVEL'INV*'     OLOBJ     P
C                           MOVEL'*FILE'    OLTYP     P
C                           EXSR OBJLST
```

You'll notice we've sized the user space fairly large — at 50,000 bytes. Although list APIs automatically extend a user space when it becomes full, extents are very slow; so it's a good idea to create a large user space to keep extents to a minimum.

After the program performs the code above, the user space contains the list of files found and — as all user spaces do — a generic user space header that provides details (e.g., list length and number of list entries) about the list information retrieved. Now all you have to do is traverse the user space, reading each entry. To do this, you first use subroutine ULHRTV (Figure 27.4) to retrieve the generic header for the user space.

FIGURE 27.4
ULHRTV Retrieve User Space List Header

```
... 1 ...+... 2 ...+... 3 ...+... 4 ...+... 5 ...+... 6 ...+... 7 ...+... 8
*----------------------------------------------------------------------
* ULHRTV - Retrieve User Space List Header function
*
* Function:
*   Retrieves the list header from a user space created by an
*   IBM compatible List API. Use the USCRT function to create
*   the user space, and a List API to load it. Use the ULERTV
*   function to retrieve the list entries after running this
*   function.
*
* Requires copy modules:
*   ULDS   - Data structure for User Space List functions
*   USDS   - Data structures for User Space functions
*
* Expects:
*   USQNAM - user_space_qual_name:
*     USNAM  - user_space_name
*     USLIB  - user_space_lib
*
```

continued

FIGURE 27.4 CONTINUED

```
... 1 ...+... 2 ...+... 3 ...+... 4 ...+... 5 ...+... 6 ...+... 7 ...+... 8
 * Returns:
 *   ULDS    - user_space_list_header_DS, including:
 *     ULEOCR - user_space_entry_occurs
 *     ULESIZ - user_space_entry_size
 *   ULEPTR - user_space_entry_ptr (to first entry)
 *   ERRDS  - err_API_DS
 *
 * Example:
 *   Retrieve the list header for the user space MYSPC in
 *   library MYLIB. The function returns the following data
 *   for input to Retrieve User Space List Entry function
 *   RTVULE: MLEPTR points to the first list entry; MLESIZ
 *   is the size of an entry; MLEOCR is the number of
 *   occurrences in the list.
 *
C*                        MOVEL'MYSPC'  USNAM     P
C*                        MOVEL'MYLIB'  USLIB     P
C*                        EXSR ULHRTV
C*                        Z-ADDULEPTR   MLEPTR
C*                        Z-ADDULESIZ   MLESIZ
C*                        Z-ADDULEOCR   MLEOCR
 *
 *-----------------------------------------------------------------
C         ULHRTV          BEGSR
 *
C         *LIKE           DEFN ULLOFF   ULEPTR
 *
C                         Z-ADDULHPTR   USPTR
C                         Z-ADDULHLEN   USLEN
 *
C                         CALL 'QUSRTVUS'
C                         PARM          USQNAM
C                         PARM          USPTR
C                         PARM          USLEN
C                         PARM          ULDS
C                         PARM          ERRDS
 *
C         ULLOFF          ADD  1        ULEPTR
 *
C                         ENDSR
```

In the code below, three fields are used to store the values we need to process the entries in the list: OLEPTR points to the first entry in the list, OLESIZ defines the size of each entry, OLEOCR defines the number of occurrences of the list. Routine ULHRTV retrieves this information from the user space header.

```
 * Initialize list variables for routine ULHRTV
C         *LIKE           DEFN ULEPTR   OLEPTR
C         *LIKE           DEFN ULESIZ   OLESIZ
C         *LIKE           DEFN ULEOCR   OLEOCR
 *
 * Specify the user space to read
C                         MOVEL'OBJUS'  USNAM     P
C                         MOVEL'QTEMP'  USLIB     P
 * Read the user space header
C                         EXSR ULHRTV
```

```
C                              Z-ADDULEPTR    OLEPTR
C                              Z-ADDULESIZ    OLESIZ
C                              Z-ADDULEOCR    OLEOCR
```

Finally, you use the ULERTV subroutine (Figure 27.5) with the three fields
returned from the generic header to retrieve each entry in the list.

FIGURE 27.5

ULERTV Retrieve User Space List Entry Function

```
... 1 ...+... 2 ...+... 3 ...+... 4 ...+... 5 ...+... 6 ...+... 7 ...+... 8
 *   ULDS   - Data structure for User Space List functions
 *   USDS   - Data structures for User Space functions
 *
 * Expects:
 *   USQNAM - user_space_qual_name:
 *     USNAM  - user_space_name
 *     USLIB  - user_space_lib
 *   ULESIZ - user_space_entry_size
 *   ULEPTR - user_space_entry_ptr (to current entry)
 *
 * Returns:
 *   UDDS   - user_space_data_DS
 *   ULEPTR - user_space_entry_ptr (to next entry)
 *   ERRDS  - err_API_DS
 *
 * Example:
 *   Retrieve the entries from the user space MYSPC in library
 *   MYLIB and move them to the member description data
 *   structure MDDS for processing. Uses the following data
 *   returned by RTVULH: MLEPTR points to the next list entry;
 *   MLESIZ is the size of an entry; MLEOCR is the number of
 *   occurrences in the list.
 *
C*          1          DO   MLEOCR    MLEIDX
 *
C*                     MOVEL'MYSPC'   USNAM      P
C*                     MOVEL'MYLIB'   USLIB      P
C*                     Z-ADDMLEPTR    ULEPTR
C*                     Z-ADDMLESIZ    ULESIZ
C*                     EXSR ULERTV
C*                     MOVELUDDS      MLDS
C*                     Z-ADDULEPTR    MLEPTR
 *                     ...
C*                     ENDDO
 *
 *-------------------------------------------------------------------
C           ULERTV     BEGSR
 *
C                      Z-ADDULEPTR    USPTR
C                      Z-ADDULESIZ    USLEN
 *
C                      CALL 'QUSRTVUS'
C                      PARM           USQNAM
C                      PARM           USPTR
C                      PARM           USLEN
C                      PARM           UDDS
C                      PARM           ERRDS
 *
C                      ADD  ULESIZ    ULEPTR
 *
C                      ENDSR
```

As the code below demonstrates, on each iteration of the loop, a list entry is retrieved and moved to OBJDS for processing, and OLEPTR is updated to point to the next entry in the loop.

```
C               *LIKE      DEFN OLEOCR    OLEIDX
 *
 * For every entry in the list, do...
C               1          DO   OLEOCR    OLEIDX
C                          MOVEL'OBJUS'   USNAM      P
C                          MOVEL'QTEMP'   USLIB      P
C                          Z-ADDOLEPTR    ULEPTR
C                          Z-ADDOLESIZ    ULESIZ
 * Retrieve an entry putting the information
 * retrieved in the OBJDS data structure (shown in
 * Figure 27.1)
C                          EXSR ULERTV
C                          MOVELUDDS      OBJDS
C                          Z-ADDULEPTR    OLEPTR
C        :                 process entry
C                          ENDDO
```

You may wonder why we bother copying the fields ULEPTR, ULESIZ, and ULECUR to their OLE*xxx* counterparts, when we could just pass the ULE*xxx* fields from subroutine ULHRTV to ULERTV. The reason is twofold. First, using two sets of fields makes the code snippets above more readable by showing the dependencies between the two subroutines. Second, the code is easier to extend. For example, we could use the Retrieve Member List API to list the members in each file returned by the List Object API without risk of the ULE*xxx* fields for the member list corrupting those for the object list. It's well worth the trouble to pay attention to such minor details when you code, because doing so makes your programs easier to enhance.

A thorough discussion of user spaces and using the list APIs is beyond the scope of this book. However, the code provided in Chapter 26 and in this chapter and an hour or two spent with the *System API Reference*, should make using the list APIs much easier for you.

Chapter 28

File Maintenance Without Record Locks

Use the following technique to write safe and robust file maintenance programs that don't lock records while they are displayed to the user.

Perhaps owing to legacy RPG limitation (i.e., its previous inability to read an unlocked record from an update file), many RPG maintenance programs always lock a record while it is displayed for the user to change. The up side is that data integrity is preserved because no other job on the system can change the locked record. The down side is that any other job trying to update the record must wait until it is released. Real problems arise when the "other" job is a critical batch update that bombs because the wait-for-file value on the file's description is reached and the job terminates abnormally. In this chapter we show you an alternative approach to maintaining files that keeps the up side and gets rid of the down side. The technique, reading files with No Intention To Update, is called NITU for short.

With the NITU approach, three buffers are used to store the entire contents of any record that needs updating. One buffer is used to store a "snapshot" of the record before the operator makes changes, one buffer is used to save a snapshot of the the operator's changes, and a third buffer contains the record contents as it is read from disk a second time. The following pseudodocode shows NITU in action:

```
Read unlocked Record A into CurrentBuffer
OldBuffer = CurrentBuffer
Make changes as needed to CurrentBuffer
NewBuffer = CurrentBuffer
Reread locked Record A into CurrentBuffer
If Record A deleted then
  Display record deleted message
Else
If CurrentBuffer <> OldBuffer then
  Display record changed since first read message
  Unlock Record A
Else
  Update Record A with NewBuffer contents
EndIf
```

If another job has updated the record, you treat the user's changes as an error, and display a message to that effect. You could add logic to the algorithm to enable the user to press F5 to refresh the data displayed and rekey his or her changes to the new version displayed.

Let's look at how to apply the NITU pseudocode to RPG in a typical file maintenance program. The program maintains an Item Master file (ITMMST), with record format ITMMSTR, keyed on item number (IMITM). The F-specs define ITMMST as an update file:

```
FITMMST  UF  E              K        DISK                                  A
```

The I-specs include three data structures to store copies of the INVMSTR record format:

```
IEDTDS      EIDSITMMST                  9999
IOLDDS       IDS                        9999
INEWDS       IDS                        9999
```

The EDTDS data structure uses the external definition of the INVMST file to store the data from a record. The OLDDS and NEWDS data structures are used as temporary storage areas for a record. (From our pseudocode, EDTDS corresponds to the CurrentBuffer, OLDDS corresponds to the OldBuffer, and NEWDS corresponds to the NewBuffer). Note how all the data structures are defined as 9,999 bytes long, rather than with the actual record length of the INVMST file. This buffer length independence is so that the program can simply be recompiled if new fields are added to the file.

When a record is selected for maintenance, it is read with no-lock specified on the CHAIN operation (by putting an N in column 53), and the contents of the file are saved to the OLDDS data structure:

```
 * Read record to update with no lock
C           IMKEY     CHAINITMMST                    N99
 * Save current record contents to OldBuffer
C                     MOVE EDTDS        OLDDS
```

The contents of the record are then displayed for the user to change.

After the user makes any changes and presses Enter, the data is then validated as normal. If no errors occur with the new field values, the following code is executed:

```
 * Field values have been validated, attempt update
 *
 * Save modified field values to NewBuffer
C                     MOVE EDTDS        NEWDS
 * Reread record with lock this time
C           IMKEY     CHAINITMMST                     99
 *
C                     SELEC
 *
C           *IN99     WHEQ *ON
 * Display record deleted message
   :
C           EDTDS     WHNE OLDDS
 * Display record changed since first read message
   :
C                     UNLCKITMMST
 * Put modified values back in CurrentBuffer
```

```
 * (perhaps to redisplay to the user)
C                         MOVE NEWDS      EDTDS
   :
C                         OTHER
 * Update record with NewBuffer contents
C                         MOVE NEWDS      EDTDS
C                         UPDATITMMSTR
   :
C                         ENDSL
```

The data returned from the display file is saved to the NEWDS data structure. The INVMST record is then read and locked. If the record is not found, then another job has deleted it. If the record just read (in EDTDS) is different from the one displayed (in OLDDS), then another job has changed it; so the record is unlocked and the user's changes in NEWDS are restored to EDTDS. When no errors are found, the user's changes are restored and the record updated.

You can use the code snippet above as the basis for checking additions and deletions. For an addition, if the record already exists, it has been added by another job, and the current record must be unlocked and an error displayed. For a deletion, if the record no longer exists, it has been deleted by another job, and an error message should be displayed. With additional buffers, this technique also can easily be adapted to applications that update records from more than one file with each display screen.

As you can see, the NITU technique requires very little coding and can greatly improve the robustness of your file maintenance programs. The code's simplicity is due primarily to RPG's ability to compare or move entire data structures with a single operation. This is a powerful feature of RPG for which you will find many other uses.

Appendix A

Getting the Most from /COPY

Much of this book's code is presented as /COPY modules. This appendix outlines a strategy for using /COPY modules in your production code.

Many RPG programs contain duplicate code. When it's not practical to split the duplicate code into a called program, move it to a separate member you can include in your programs at compilation using RPG's /COPY statement. The /COPY statement is coded from position 7 of a source line and has the following format:

```
/COPY SRCLIB/SRCFIL,MBR
```

Both the source library and file are optional, allowing you to code just the member name:

```
/COPY MBR
```

When only the member name is specified, the RPG compiler searches all QRPGSRC source files in your library list to locate the member. This shorthand approach is very powerful, because the /COPY statement is not bound to a specific file and library. You can change the entries in your library list to compile programs with different versions of copy members for testing. You can also use QRPGSRC in different libraries for different types of copy members. For example, QRPGSRC in GENLIB might contain general routines you can use in any program, while QRPGSRC in INVLIB might contain routines for your inventory application. For application-specific copy members, it is a good idea to prefix member names with the identifier for the application, so all inventory copy members start with INV.

To make /COPY members really useful demands a little thought. Each copy member should include a header section that defines the function of the member, all input and output fields, and any dependent copy members that also must be included for compilation. /COPY members also must be thoroughly tested to make sure they work properly. However, if you do find a bug in one, you just edit the member and then use PDM's "find string" option to find and recompile all the affected programs.

/COPY lets you code faster, and maintain programs more easily, by focusing on the specifics of a program and storing reusable code in one central repository. Good candidates for copy members include commonly used data structures, field names, named constants, parameter lists, and low-level subroutines.

TYPOS   11-26-96 ℔

p. 188   ACO instead of ACQ

p. 49   387 instead of 382-383

p. 46   why no HOME key?

Appendix B

String Functions Test Program

Ensure that your libraries of reusable RPG routines work correctly by building interactive test programs.

When you build libraries of RPG functions, such as the string functions we presented in Chapters 16–19, you'll always want to test those functions thoroughly before you use them in production programs. When we build such libraries, we build test programs such as the one presented in this appendix. As you build your reusable libraries of RPG code, don't discount the value of building such testing programs. The time invested up front to build test programs like this pays off handsomely in the end.

To interactively test the 12 string functions presented in Chapters 16–19, use RPG program TSTSTR, (Figure B.1) and display file TSTSTRD (Figure B.2). You'll find that experimenting with TSTSTR quickly adds to your understanding of the string functions and how they work. Compile instructions are included as comments in Figure B.1.

FIGURE B.1
TSTSTRD RPG Program (Test String Functions)

```
*------------------------------------------------------------------
* TSTSTR - Test string functions
*------------------------------------------------------------------
*
* Function:
*   Allows you to interactively test the twelve string functions
*   presented in Chapters 16-19.
*
* To compile:
*   1. Create the display file shown in Figure B.2 with CRTDSPF
*
*   2. Ensure that members:
*        WSDS          WSCONS        STRDS         STDCONST
*        STRCAT        STRCTR        STRFND        STRFNL
*        STRLAJ        STRLEN        STRLWR        STRPAD
*        STRRAJ        STRSUB        STRTRM        STRUPR
*      are all available in a QRPGSRC source file. If you have
*      these members in a source file with a different name,
*      you'll need to qualify the /COPY references with the
*      appropriate source file name.
*
*   3. Compile this program with CRTRPGPGM
*------------------------------------------------------------------
FTSTSTRD CF  E                    WORKSTN      KINFDS WSDS
*
I/COPY WSDS
I/COPY WSCONS
```

continued

FIGURE B.1 CONTINUED

```
... 1 ...+... 2 ...+... 3 ...+... 4 ...+... 5 ...+... 6 ...+... 7 ...+... 8
 *
I/COPY STRDS
I/COPY STDCONST
 *
C           *ON        DOWEQ*ON
 *
C                      EXFMTTSTSTRR
 *
C           WSKEY      IFEQ WSF03
C           WSKEY      OREQ WSF12
C                      LEAVE
C                      ENDIF
 *
C           SUITE      CASEQ'STRCAT'    STRCAT
C           SUITE      CASEQ'STRCTR'    STRCTR
C           SUITE      CASEQ'STRFND'    STRFND
C           SUITE      CASEQ'STRFNL'    STRFNL
C           SUITE      CASEQ'STRLAJ'    STRLAJ
C           SUITE      CASEQ'STRLEN'    STRLEN
C           SUITE      CASEQ'STRLWR'    STRLWR
C           SUITE      CASEQ'STRPAD'    STRPAD
C           SUITE      CASEQ'STRRAJ'    STRRAJ
C           SUITE      CASEQ'STRSUB'    STRSUB
C           SUITE      CASEQ'STRTRM'    STRTRM
C           SUITE      CASEQ'STRUPR'    STRUPR
C                      CAS              STRX
C                      ENDCS
 *
C                      ENDDO
 *
C                      MOVE *ON         *INLR
 *
C           STRX       BEGSR
C                      MOVE *ON         STRERR
C                      Z-ADD*HIVAL      STRP
C                      ENDSR
 *
C/COPY STRCAT
C/COPY STRCTR
C/COPY STRFND
C/COPY STRFNL
C/COPY STRLAJ
C/COPY STRLEN
C/COPY STRLWR
C/COPY STRPAD
C/COPY STRRAJ
C/COPY STRSUB
C/COPY STRTRM
C/COPY STRUPR
```

FIGURE **B.2**
Display File TSTSTRD

```
... 1 ...+... 2 ...+... 3 ...+... 4 ...+... 5 ...+... 6 ...+... 7 ...+... 8
*-----------------------------------------------------------------
* TSTSTRD - Test string functions display file DDS
*-----------------------------------------------------------------
A                                      DSPSIZ(24 80 *DS3)
A                                      PRINT
A                                      INDTXT(60 'SFLCLR')
A                                      INDTXT(61 'SFLDSP')
A                                      INDTXT(62 'SFLDSPCTL')
A                                      INDTXT(63 'SFLEND')
A                                      INDTXT(64 'SFLINZ')
A                                      INDTXT(65 'SFLNXTCHG')
A                                      INDTXT(66 'SFLBOF')
A                                      INDTXT(70 'Record was changed')
A                                      INDTXT(71 'Protect Fields')
A                                      INDTXT(72 'Non-display Fields')
A                                      INDTXT(73 'SFLFOLD')
A                                      INDTXT(75 'Valid Command Key')
A                                      INDTXT(76 'Error in Entry')
A           R TSTSTRR
A                                      TEXT('Test string functions')
A                                      CA03
A                                      CA12
A                                      CHANGE(70)
A                                      VLDCMDKEY(75)
A                                      OVERLAY
A                                      RTNDTA
A                                      RTNCSRLOC(&FICRN &FICFN &FICPOS)
A             FICRN      10A   H       TEXT('Cursor Record Name')
A             FICFN      10A   H       TEXT('Cursor Field Name')
A             FICPOS      4S  0H       TEXT('Cursor Position')
A                                  1  2'TSTSTR'
A                                      COLOR(BLU)
A                                  1 35'String Tests'
A                                      DSPATR(HI)
A                                  3  2'Type information, press Enter.'
A                                      COLOR(BLU)
A                                  5  2'SUITE :'
A             SUITE       6A   B  5 10
A                                  7  2'STR1  :'
A             STR1      256A   B  8  1
A                                 12  2'STR1LN:'
A             STR1LN      3S  0B 12 10
A                                 12 22'STR1PS:'
A             STR1PS      3S  0B 12 30
A                                 12 42'STR1SZ:'
A             STR1SZ      3S  0B 12 50
A                                 14  2'STR2  :'
A             STR2      256A   B 15  1
A                                 19  2'STR2LN:'
A             STR2LN      3S  0B 19 10
A                                 19 22'STR2PS:'
A             STR2PS      3S  0B 19 30
A                                 19 42'STR2SZ:'
A             STR2SZ      3S  0B 19 50
A                                 21  2'STRERR:'
A             STRERR      1A   O 21 10
A                                 21 22'STRP  :'
A             STRP        3Y  0O 21 30EDTCDE(J)
A                                 23  2'F3=Exit'
A                                      COLOR(BLU)
A                                 23 13'F12=Cancel'
A                                      COLOR(BLU)
```

Appendix C

RPG Reference

CONTROL SPECIFICATIONS (H-SPECS)

Position	Name	Entry
1–5	Sequence	Sequence identifier
6	Form type	H
7 - 14		
15	Debug	Blank, 1
16–17		
18	Currency symbol	Blank, currency symbol
19	Date format	Blank, M, D, Y
20	Date edit	Blank, any character
21	Decimal notation	Blank, I, J, D
22–25		
26	Alternate collating sequence	Blank, S
27–39		
40	Sign handling	Blank
41	Forms alignment	Blank, 1
42		
43	File translation	Blank, F44–56
55	Subprogram	Blank, S
57	Transparency check	Blank, 1
58–74		
75–80	Program identification	Program name

FILE SPECIFICATIONS (F-SPECS)

Main File Description Line Summary

Position	Name	Entry
1–5	Sequence	Sequence identifier
6	Form type	F
7–14	File name	File name
15	File type	I, O, U, C
16	File designation	Blank, P, S, R, T, F
17	End of file	Blank, E
18	Sequence	Blank, A, D
19	File format	F, E
20–23		
24–27	Record length	1–9999
28	Limits processing	Blank, L
29–30	Key length or record address field	Blank, 1–99
31	Record address type	Blank, A, P, K
32	File organization	Blank, I, T
33–34	Overflow indicators	Blank, OA–OG, OV, 01–99
35–38	Key field start location	Blank, 1–9999
39	Extension code	Blank, E, L
40–46	Device	PRINTER, DISK, WORKSTN, SPECIAL, SEQ
47–52		
53	Continuation lines	Blank, K
54–59	Routine name	Name of user routine
60–65		
66	File addition/unordered	Blank, A
67–70		
71–72	File condition	Blank, U1–U8, UC
73–74		
75–80	Comments	Optional

Continuation Line Summary

Position	Name	Entry
1–5	Sequence	Sequence identifier
6	Form type	F
7–18		
19–28		External name of record format
29–46		
47–52	Record number field for SFILE	Numeric field name
53	Continuation line	K
54–59, 60–67[1]		
68–74		
75–80	Comments	Optional

[1]These positions are used together (see below). Positions 54–59 specify the option, while positions 60–67 further explain the option.

CONTINUATION LINE OPTIONS SUMMARY

Option (54–59)	Entry (60–67)	Explanation
COMIT		This file is specified for commitment control.
ID	Field name	Positions 60–65 contain the left-justified name of a 10-character alphanumeric field that requires no further definition. This field contains the name of the program device that supplied the record being processed in the file.
IGNORE		This option lets you ignore a record format from an externally described file.
IND	Indicator number	Indicators from 01 to the specified number are saved and restored for each device attached to a mixed — or multiple — device file.
INFDS	Data structure name	This entry lets you define and name a data structure to contain the exception/error information. The data structure name is entered in positions 60–65 and left-justified. If you specify INFDS for more than one file, each associated data structure must have a unique name.

continued

CONTINUATION LINE OPTIONS SUMMARY, *CONTINUED*

Option (54–59)	Entry (60–67)	Explanation
NFSR	Subroutine name	The file exception/error subroutine named (left-justified) in positions 60–65 may receive control after file exceptions/ errors. The subroutine name *PSSR indicates that the user-defined program exception/error subroutine is to receive control for errors on this file.
NUM	Maximum number of devices	The specified number must be greater than zero and right–justified in positions 60–65.
PASS	*NOIND	Specify PASS *NOIND on the F-specification continuation line for a program described WORKSTN file if you are taking responsibility for passing indicators on input and output.
PLIST	Parameter list name	This entry is valid only when the device specified in positions 40–46 of the main file description line is SPECIAL. Positions 60–65 give the left-justified name of the parameter list that is to be passed to the special routine.
PRTCTL	Data structure name	The dynamic printer-control option is being used. The data structure specified left-justified in positions 60–65 refers to the forms-control information and line-count value.
RECNO	Field name	This entry is optional for disk files to be processed by relative record number (RRN). A RECNO field must be specified for output files processed by RRN, output files referenced by a random WRITE calculation operation, or output files used with ADD on the output specifications.
RENAME	Record format name	This optional entry lets you rename record formats in an externally described file. Positions 19–28 of the continuation line specify the external name of the record format that is to be renamed. Positions 60–67 specify the left-justified name of the record as it is used in the program.
SAVDS	Data structure name	Positions 60–65 contain the left-justiied name of the data structure that is saved and restored for each device.
SFILE	Record format name	Positions 60–67 must specify, left-justified, the RPG name of the record format to be processed as a subfile. Positions 47–52 must specify the name of the relative record number field for this subfile.
SLN	Field name	Positions 60–65 contain the left-justified name of a start line number (SLN) field. The SLN field determines where a record format will be written to a display file.

EXTENSION SPECIFICATIONS (E-SPECS)

Position	Name	Entry
1–5	Sequence	Sequence identifier
6	Form type	E
7–10		
11–18	From file name	Blank, record-address file name, array, or table file name
19–26	To file name	Blank, name of an input or update file containing data records, name of an output or combined file
27–32	Table or array name	Table or array name
33–35	Number of entries per record	Blank, 1–999
36–39	Number of entries per array or table	1–9999
40–42	Length of entry	1–256
43	Data format	Blank, P, B, L, R
44	Decimal positions	Blank, 0–9
45	Sequence	Blank, A, D
46–51	Table or array name	Table or array name (alternating format)
52–54	Length of entry	1–256
55	Data format	Blank, P, B, L, R
56	Decimal positions	Blank, 0–9
57	Sequence	Blank, A, D
58–80	Comments	Optional

LINE COUNTER SPECIFICATIONS (L-SPECS)

Position	Name	Entry
1–5	Sequence	Sequence identifier
6	Form type	L
7–14	File name	File name
15–17	Number of lines per page	2–112
18–19	Form length	FL
20–22	Overflow line number	2–112
23–24	Overflow line	OL
25–74		
75–80	Comments	Optional

INPUT SPECIFICATIONS (I-SPECS)

Externally Described Files, Record-Identification Entries

Position	Name	Entry
1–5	Sequence	Sequence identifier
6	Form type	I
7–14	Record name	Record format name
15–18		
19–20	Record-identifying indicators	Blank, 01–99, L1–L9, LR, H1–H9, U1–U8, RT
21–74		
75–80	Comments	Optional

Externally Described Files, Field Entries

Position	Name	Entry
1–5	Sequence	Sequence identifier
6	Form type	I
7–20		
21–30	External field name	Field name
31–52		
53–58	RPG field name	Field name
59–60	Control level	Blank, L1–L9
61–62	Match fields	Blank, M1–M9
63–64		
65–70	Field indicators	Blank, 01–99, H1–H9, U1–U8, RT
71–74		
75–80	Comments	Optional

Program-Described Files, Record-Identification Entries

Position	Name	Entry
1–5	Sequence	Sequence identifier
6	Form type	I
7–14	File name	File name
14–16	Logical relationship	AND or OR
15–16	Sequence	Any two alphabetic characters, any 2-digit number
17	Number	Blank, 1, N
18	Option	Blank, O
19–20	Record-identifying indicators	01–99, L1–L9, LR, H1–H9, U1–U8, RT, **
21–24, 28–31, 35–38	Position	Blank, 1–9999
25, 32, 39	Logical relationship	Blank, N
26, 33, 40	Code part	C, Z, D
27, 34, 41	Character	Any character
42–74		
75–80	Comments	Optional

Program-Described Files, Field-Description Entries

Position	Name	Entry
1–5	Sequence	Sequence identifier
6	Form type	I
7–42		
43	Data format	Blank, P, B, L, R
44–47	From	1–9999
48–51	To	1–9999
52	Decimal positions	Blank, 0–9
53–58	Field name	Symbolic name
59–60	Control level	Blank, L1–L9
61–62	Match fields	Blank, M1–M9
63–64	Field record relation	Blank, 01–99, L1–L9, MR, U1–U8, H1–H9, RT
65–70	Field indicators	Blank, 01–99, H1–H9, U1–U8, RT
71–74		
75–80	Comments	Optional

Data-Structure Statement Specifications

Position	Name	Entry
1–5	Sequence	Sequence identifier
6	Form type	I
7–12	Data structure name	Blank, data structure name
13–16		
17	External description	Blank, E
18	Option	Blank, I, S, U
19–20	Record-identifying indicators	DS
21–30	External file name	External name of data structure
31–43		
44–47	Occurrences	Blank, 1–9999
48–51	Data structure length	Blank, 1–9999
52–74		
75–80	Comments	Optional

Data-Structure Subfield Specifications

Position	Name	Entry
1–5	Sequence	Sequence identifier
6	Form type	I
7–20		
8	Initialization option	Blank, I
9–20		
21–30	External field name	External name of subfield
21–42	Initialization value	Initial value
31–42		
43	Data format	Blank, P, B
44–47	From	1–9999
48–51	To	1–9999
44–51	Keywords	Keywords
52	Decimal positions	Blank, 0–9
53–58	Subfield name	Subfield name
59–74		
75–80	Comments	Optional

Named-Constant Specifications

Position	Name	Entry
1–5	Sequence	Sequence identifier
6	Form type	I
7–20		
21–42	Constant	Constant value
43	Data type	Blank, C
44–52		
53–58	Constant name	Name
59–74		
75–80	Comments	Optional

CALCULATION SPECIFICATIONS (C-SPECS)

Position	Name	Entry
1–5	Sequence	Sequence identifier
6	Form type	C
7–8	Control level	Blank, L0, L1–L9, LR, SR, AN, OR
9–17	Conditioning indicators	Blank, 01–99, KA–KN, KP–KY, L1–L9, LR, MR, H1–H9, RT, U1–U8, OA–OG, OV
18–27	Factor 1	Symbolic name or literal
28–32	Operation	Opcode
33–42	Factor 2	Symbolic name or literal
43–48	Result field	Field name
49–51	Field length	Blank, 1–15, 1–30, 1–256
52	Decimal positions	Blank, 0–9
53	Operation extender	Blank, P, H, N
54–59	Resulting indicators	Blank, 01–99, KA–KN, KP–KY, H1–H9, L1–L9, LR, OA–OG, OV, U1–U8, RT
60–80	Comments	Optional

OUTPUT SPECIFICATIONS (O-SPECS)

Externally Described Files, Record-Identification and Control Entries

Position	Name	Entry
1–5	Sequence	Sequence identifier
6	Form type	O
7–14	Record name	Record–format name
14–16	Logical relationship	AND or OR
15	Type	H, D, T, E
16	Release	R
16–18	Record addition field	ADD, DEL
16–22	Space/Skip, fetch overflow	Blank
23–31	Output indicators	Blank, 01–99, KA–KN, KP–KY, L1–L9, H1–H9, U1–U8, MR, LR, RT, 1P
32–37	EXCPT name	Record group name
38–74		
75–80	Comments	Optional

Externally Described Files, Field-Description and Control Entries

Position	Name	Entry
1–5	Sequence	Sequence identifier
6	Form type	O
7–22		
23–31	Field output indicators	See output indicators
32–37	Field name	Field name, *ALL
38		
39	Blank after	Blank, B
40–74		
75–80	Comments	Optional

Program-Described Files, Record-Identification and Control Entries (Record Line)

Position	Name	Entry
1–5	Sequence	Sequence identifier
6	Form type	O
7–14	File name	File name
14–16	AND/OR	AND or OR
15	Type	H, D, T, E
16–18	ADD/DEL	ADD, DEL
16	Fetch overflow; Release	Blank, F, or R
17	Space before	Blank, 0, 1, 2, 3
18	Space after	Blank, 0, 1, 2, 3
19–20	Skip before	1–99, A0–A9, B0–B2
21–22	Skip after	1–99, A0–A9, B0–B2
23–31	Output indicators	Blank, 1–99, KA–KN, KP–KY, L1–L9, H1–H9, U1–U8, OA–OG, OV, MR, LR, RT, 1P
32–37	EXCPT name	Record group name
38–74		
75–80	Comments	Optional

Program-Described Files, Field-Description and Control Entries (Field Line)

Position	Name	Entry
1–5	Sequence	Sequence identifier
6	Form type	O
7–22		
23–31	Field output indicators	See output indicators
32–37	Field name	Field name, PAGE, PAGE1–PAGE7, UDATE, UDAY, UMONTH, UYEAR, *DATE, *DAY, *MONTH, *YEAR, *PLACE
38	Edit code	Blank, 1–4, 5–9, A–D, J–Q, X, Y, Z
39	Blank after	Blank, B
40–43	End position in output record	Blanks, +nnn, -nnn, nnnn, K1–K8
44	Data format	Blank, P, B, L, R, G
45–70	Constant or edit word	Constant or edit word, format name
71–74		
75–80	Comments	Optional

OPCODES

- An empty column indicates that the field must be blank or that there is no resulting indicator in that position.
- All underlined fields are required.
- Symbols:

(h)	Half adjust the result
(n)	Do not lock record on input if file is update
(p)	Pad the result with blanks
+	Plus
–	Minus
BL	Blank(s)
BN	Blank(s) then numeric
BOF	Beginning of file
EOF	End of file
EQ	Equal
ER	Error
FD	Found
HI	Greater than
IN	Indicator
LO	Less than
LR	Last record
NR	No record found
NU	Numeric
OF	Off
ON	On
Z	Zero
ZB	Zero or blank

Opcode Specifications

Codes	Factor 1	Factor 2	Result Field	Resulting Indicators		
ACO	Device name	WORKSTN file			ER	
ADD (h)	Addend	Addend	Sum	+	–	Z
ANDxx	Comparand	Comparand				

continued

Opcode Specifications, *CONTINUED*

Codes	Factor 1	Factor 2	Result Field	Resulting Indicators		
BEGSR	Subroutine name					
BITOF		Bit numbers	Character field			
BITON		Bit numbers	Character field			
CABxx	Comparand	Comparand	Label	HI	LO	EQ
CALL		Program name	PLIST name		ER	LR
CASxx	Comparand	Comparand	Subroutine name	HI	LO	EQ
CAT (p)	Source string 1	Source string 2: number of blanks	Target string			
CHAIN (n) argument	Search record name	File name or	Data structure	NR	ER	
CHECK[1]	Comparator	Base string:start	Leftmost position(s)		ER	FD
CHEKR[1]	Comparator string	Base string:start	Rightmost position(s)		ER	FD
CLEAR	*NOKEY	Structure or variable or record name				
CLOSE		File name			ER	
COMIT	Boundary				ER	
COMP[2]	Comparand	Comparand		HI	LO	EQ
DEBUG	Identifier	Output file	Debug information			
DEFN	*LIKE	Referenced field	Defined field			
DEFN	*NAMVAR or *EXTRN	External data area	Internal program area			
DELET	Search argument	File name		NR	ER	
DIV (h)	Dividend	Divisor	Quotient	+	−	Z
DO	Starting value	Limit value	Index value			
DOUxx	Comparand	Comparand				
DOWxx	Comparand	Comparand				

continued

Opcode Specifications, *CONTINUED*

Codes	Factor 1	Factor 2	Result Field	Resulting Indicators		
DSPLY	Message identifier	Output queue	Response		ER	
DUMP	Identifier					
ELSE						
END		Increment value				
ENDCS						
ENDDO		Increment value				
ENDIF						
ENDSL						
ENDSR	Label	Return point				
EXCPT		EXCPT name				
EXFMT		Record format name			ER	
EXSR		Subroutine name				
FEOD		File name			ER	
FORCE		File name				
FREE		Program name			ER	
GOTO		Label				
Ifxx	Comparand	Comparand				
IN	*LOCK	Data area name			ER	
ITER						
KFLD			Key field			
KLIST	KLIST name					
LEAVE						
LOKUP[2]						
(array)	Search argument	Array name		HI	LO	EQ
(table)	Search argument	Table name	Table name	HI	LO	EQ

continued

Opcode Specifications, *CONTINUED*

Codes	Factor 1	Factor 2	Result Field	Resulting Indicators		
MHHZO		Source field	Target field			
MHLZO		Source field	Target field			
MLHZO		Source field	Target field			
MLLZO		Source field	Target field			
MOVE (p)		Source field	Target field	+	−	ZB
MOVEA (p)		Source	Target	+	−	ZB
MOVEL (p)		Source field	Target field	+	−	ZB
MULT (h)	Multiplicand	Multiplier	Product	+	−	Z
MVR			Remainder	+	−	Z
NEXT	Program device	File name			ER	
OCCUR	Occurrence value	Data structure	Occurrence value		ER	
OPEN		File name			ER	
Orxx	Comparand	Comparand				
OTHER						
OUT	*LOCK	Data area name			ER	
PARM	Target field	Source field	Parameter			
PLIST	PLIST name					
POST[3]	Program device	File name or record name	INFDS name		ER	
READ (n)		File name or record name	Data structure		ER	EOF
READC		Record name			ER	EOF
READE (n)	Search argument	File name or record name	Data structure		ER	EOF
READP (n)		File name or record name	Data structure		ER	BOF
REDPE (n)	Search argument	File name or record name	Data structure		ER	BOF
REL	Program device	File name			ER	
RESET	*NOKEY	Structure or variable or variable name			ER	

continued

Opcode Specifications, *CONTINUED*

Codes	Factor 1	Factor 2	Result Field	Resulting Indicators		
RETRN						
ROLBK				ER		
SCAN 2	Comparator string:length	Base string: start	Leftmost position(s)		ER	FD
SELEC						
SETGT	Search argument	File name or record name		NR	ER	
SETLL	Search argument	File name or record name		NR	ER	EQ
SETOF[2]			OF	OF	OF	
SETON[2]			ON	ON	ON	
SHTDN			ON			
SORTA		Array name				
SQRT (h)		Value	Root			
SUB (h)	Minuend	Subtrahend	Difference	+	−	Z
SUBST (p)	Length to extract	Base string:unit	Target string		ER	
TAG	Label					
TESTB[2]		Bit numbers	Character field	OF	ON	EQ
TESTN[2]		Character field	NU	BN	BL	
TESTZ[2]		Character field				
TIME		Numeric field				
UNLCK		Data area or file name		ER		
UPDAT		File name or record name	Data structure	ER		
WHxx	Comparand	Comparand				
WRITE		File name or record name	Data structure	ER	EOF	
XFOOT (h)		Array name	Sum	+	−	Z
XLATE (p)	From:To	String:start	Target string		ER	FD
Z−ADD (h)		Addend	Sum	+	−	Z
Z−SUB (h)		Subtrahend	Difference	+	−	Z

[1] A found indicator is required if the result field is not specified.

[2] At least one resulting indicator is required.

[3] You must specify Factor 2 or the result field. You may specify both.

Editing Numeric Fields

Edit Code	Commas	Decimal Point	Sign for Negative Balance	O or Blanks	I	J
1	Yes	Yes	No sign	.00 or 0	,00 or 0	0,00 or 0
2	Yes	Yes	No sign	Blanks	Blanks	Blanks
3		Yes	No sign	.00 or 0	,00 or 0	0,00 or 0
4		Yes	No sign	Blanks	Blanks	Blanks
5–9	User-defined					
A	Yes	Yes	CR	.00 or 0	,00 or 0	0,00 or 0
B	Yes	Yes	CR	Blanks	Blanks	Blanks
C		Yes	CR	.00 or 0	,00 or 0	0,00 or 0
D		Yes	CR	Blanks	Blanks	Blanks
J	Yes	Yes	– (minus)	.00 or 0	,00 or 0	0,00 or 0
K	Yes	Yes	– (minus)	Blanks	Blanks	Blanks
L		Yes	– (minus)	.00 or 0	,00 or 0	0,00 or 0
M		Yes	– (minus)	Blanks	Blanks	Blanks
N	Yes	Yes	– (floating minus)	.00 or 0	,00 or 0	0,00 or 0
O	Yes	Yes	– (floating minus)	Blanks	Blanks	Blanks
P		Yes	– (floating minus)	.00 or 0	,00 or 0	0,00 or 0
Q		Yes	– (floating minus)	Blanks	Blanks	Blanks
X[1]						
Y[2]						
Z[3]						

Note: All entries are zero-suppressed.

[1] The X edit code ensures a plus sign for positive values.

[2] The Y edit code is normally used to edit a date field with 3–9 digits. It suppresses the leftmost zeros of date fields, up to but not including the digit preceding the first separator. The Y edit code also inserts slashes (/) between the month, day, and year according to the following pattern:

nn/n
nn/nn
nn/nn/n
nn/nn/nn
nnn/nn/nn
nn/nn/nnnn Format used with M, D, or blank in position 19
nnn/nn/nnnn Format used with M, D, or blank in position 19
nnnn/nn/nn Format used with Y in position 19
nnnnn/nn/nn Format used with Y in position 19

[3] The Z edit code removes the sign (plus or minus) from a numeric field and suppresses leading zeros of a numeric field.

RPG Special Words

The following RPG reserved words have special functions in a program:

- UDATE, UDAY, UMONTH, UYEAR, *DATE, *DAY, *MONTH, and *YEAR let you access the system date, or a portion of it, for program use.
- PAGE, PAGE1–PAGE7 can be used for numbering the pages of a report, for record–sequence numbering, or for sequentially numbering output fields.
- Figurative constants (*BLANK/*BLANKS, *ZERO/*ZEROS, *HIVAL, *LOVAL, *ON/*OFF, *ALLX'x1..', and *ALL'X..') are implied literals that allow specifications without referring to length.
- *IN and *Inxx let indicators be referred to as data.
- The following reserved words define symbolic locations in the file information data structure and the program status data structure: *FILE, *OPCODE, *PARMS, *PROGRAM, *RECORD, *ROUTINE, and *STATUS.
- The following reserved words provide symbolic labels for the ENDSR operation for the file and program exception/error subroutines or for the file information data structure:

*CANCL	Cancel the program
*DETC	Detail calculations
*DETL	Detail lines
*GETIN	Get input record
*INIT	Program initialization
*OFL	Overflow lines
*TERM	Program ending
*TOTC	Total calculations
*TOTL	Total lines

- The following special words are used with opcodes: *DEFN, *ENTRY, *INZSR, *LDA, *LIKE, *LOCK, *NAMVAR, *OFF, *ON, *PDA, and *PSSR.
- The following special words are used with translation: *EQUATE and *FILE.
- *PLACE allows repetitive placement of fields in an output record.
- *ALL lets all fields defined for an externally described file be written on output.

RPG Restrictions

Function	Restriction
AN/OR lines (positions 7 and 8 of calculation specifications)	Maximum of 7 per operation
Arrays	Maximum of 200 per program
Array input record length for compile time	Maximum length is 80
Character field length	Maximum length is 256
Control fields (positions 59 and 60 of input specifications) length	Maximum length is 256
Data structure length	Maximum of 9999
Data structure occurrences	Maximum of 9999 per data structure
Edit word	Maximum length of 24 for literals or 115 for named constants
Elements in an array/table (positions 36–39 of extension specifications)	Maximum of 9999 per array/table
File	Maximum of 50 per program
Levels of nesting in structured groups	Maximum of 100
Look-ahead	Can be specified only once for a file; can be specified only for primary and secondary files
Named constant	Maximum length of 256 for character named constant, 512 for hexadecimal named constant, and 30 digits with 9 decimal positions for numeric named constant
Numeric field length	Maximum 30 digits, 9 decimal places
Overflow indicator	Only 1 unique overflow indicator can be specified per printer file
Parameters	Maximum of 255
Primary file (P in position 16 of file specifications)	Maximum of 1 per program
Printer file (PRINTER in positions 40–46 of file specifications)	Maximum of 8 per program
Printing lines per page	Maximum of 112; minimum of 2
Program status data structure	Only 1 allowed per program
Record address file (R in position 16 of file specifications)	Only 1 allowed per program
Record length for program-described file (positions 24–27 of file specifications)	Maximum length is 9999[1]
Subroutines	Maximum of 254 per program
Tables	Maximum of 200 per program
Table input record length for compile time	Maximum length is 80

[1]Any device record size restraints override this value.

ERROR HANDLING

File Error Codes – Normal Conditions

Codes	Meaning
00000	No exception/error occurred.
00002	Function key used to end display.
00011	End of file on a read (input).
00012	No record found on a CHAIN, SETGT, SETLL operation.
00013	Subfile is full on a write operation.

File Error Codes — Exception/Error Conditions

Codes	Meaning
01011	Undefined record type (input record does not match record-identifying indicator).
01021	Tried to write a record that already exists (file being used has unique keys and key is duplicate, or attempted to use duplicate relative record number to a subfile).
01031	Match field out of sequence.
01041	Array/table load sequence error.
01051	Excess entries in array/table file.
01071	Numeric sequence error.
01121	No indicator on the DDS keyword for Print key.
01122	No indicator on the DDS keyword for Roll up key.
01123	No indicator on the DDS keyword for Roll down key.
01124	No indicator on the DDS keyword for Clear key.
01125	No indicator on the DDS keyword for Help key.
01126	No indicator on the DDS keyword for Home key.
01201	Record mismatch detected on input.
01211	I/O operation to a closed file.
01215	OPEN issued to a file already open.
01216	Error on an implicit OPEN/CLOSE operation.
01217	Error on an explicit OPEN/CLOSE operation.
01218	Record already locked.
01221	Update operation attempted without a prior read.
01231	Error on SPECIAL file.

continued

File Error Codes — Exception/Error Conditions, *CONTINUED*

Codes	Meaninig
01235	Error in PRTCTL space or skip entries.
01241	Record number not found. (Record number specified in record address file is not present in file being processed.)
01251	Permanent I/O error occurred.
01255	Session or device error occurred. Recovery may be possible.
01261	Attempt to exceed maximum number of acquired devices.
01281	Operation to unacquired device.
01282	Job ending with controlled option.
01285	Attempt to acquire a device already acquired.
01286	Attempt to open shared file with SAVDS or IND options.
01287	Response to indicators overlap IND indicators.
01299	Other I/O error detected.
01331	Wait time exceeded for READ from WORKSTN file.

Program Status Codes — Normal Conditions

Codes	Meaning
00000	No exception/error occurred.
00001	Called program returned with indicator LR on.

Program Status Codes — Exception/Error Conditions

Codes	Meaning
00100	Value out of range for string operation.
00101	Negative square root.
00102	Divide by zero.
00121	Invalid array index.
00122	OCUR outside range.
00123	RESET attempted during initialization subroutine.
00202	Called program failed; halt indicator (H1–H9) not on.
00211	Program specified on CALL or FREE not found.
00221	Called program tried to use a parameter not passed to it.
00231	Called program returned with halt indicator on.

continued

Program Status Codes — Exception/Error Conditions, *CONTINUED*

Codes	Meaning
00232	Halt indicator on in this program.
00233	Halt indicator on when RETRN operation run.
00299	RPG formatted dump failed.
00333	Error on DSPLY operation.
00401	Data area specified on IN or OUT not found.
00402	*PDA not valid for non-prestart job.
00411	Data area types or lengths do not match.
00412	Data area not locked for output.
00413	Error on IN or OUT operation.
00414	User not authorized to use data area.
00415	User not authorized to change data area.
00421	Error on UNLCK operation.
00431	Data area previously locked by another program.
00432	Data area locked by program in the same process.
00907	Decimal data error (invalid digit or sign).
00970	The level numbers of the generating compiler and the runtime subroutines do not match.
09998	Internal failure in RPG compiler or in runtime subroutines.
09999	Program exception in system routine.

Note: For more detailed reference information, refer to IBM's *RPG/400 Reference* (SC09–1817).

Index

New Books in the 29th Street Press Library

THE A TO Z OF EDI, SECOND EDITION

By Nahid M. Jilovec

The A to Z of EDI, Second Edition, gives you the practical details of EDI implementation. Not only does it show you how to cost justify EDI, but it gives you job descriptions for EDI team members, detailed criteria and forms for evaluating EDI vendors, considerations for trading-partner agreements, an EDI glossary, and lists of EDI organizations and publications. And this edition includes all-new information about EDI and the Internet, system security, and auditing. 221 pages.

THE ACCOUNTING SOFTWARE HANDBOOK
Your Guide to Evaluating Vendor Applications

By Stewart McKie

This second edition of *The Technology Guide to Accounting Software* will help you understand how you can apply technologies such as client/server (or browser/server), workflow, imaging, Online Analytical Processing (OLAP), and the Internet to deliver effective accounting systems. The accompanying CD contains more than 50 profiles of selected vendors and products. Also included is a detailed step-by-step selection process to help you efficiently arrive at a vendor shortlist for your evaluation. 265 pages.

MASTERING THE AS/400, SECOND EDITION
A Practical, Hands-On Guide

By Jerry Fottral

With its utilitarian approach that stresses student participation, this introductory textbook to AS/400 concepts and facilities emphasizes mastery of system/user interface, member-object-library relationship, use of CL commands, and basic database and program development utilities. The second edition is updated to V3R1/V3R6. Each lesson includes a lab that focuses on the essential topics presented in the lesson. 575 pages.

RAPID REVIEW STUDY GUIDES

Series Editor: Mike Pastore

You know that becoming a Microsoft Certified Systems Engineer can be lucrative. Still, seeking the certification isn't a goal for the faint of heart. Our Rapid Review Study Guides give you pre- and post-assessments to measure your progress, exam preparation tips, an overview of exam material, vocabulary drills, hands-on activities, and sample quiz questions on CD and in the book. Current titles include *Networking Essentials, Windows 95, System Management Server 1.2, Windows NT 4.0 Server, TCP/IP for Microsoft Windows NT 4.0, Windows NT 4.0 Workstation, Internet Information Server 4.0,* and *Windows NT 4.0 Server in the Enterprise.*

TCP/IP AND THE AS/400

By Michael Ryan

TCP/IP and the AS/400 provides background for AS/400 professionals to understand the capabilities of TCP/IP, its strengths and weaknesses, and how to configure and administer the TCP/IP protocol stack on the AS/400. It shows TCP/IP gurus on other types of systems how to configure and manage the AS/400 TCP/IP capabilities. 362 pages.

WINDOWS NT MAGAZINE INSTANT SOLUTIONS:
TROUBLESHOOTING IIS 4.0 AND VISUAL INTERDEV 6.0

By Ken Spencer

Series editor, Sean Daily

Author Ken Spencer has worked with IIS and Visual InterDev since their early preview stages. In the first of our Instant Solutions series of books, he takes knowledge selected from his development and system management experiences and from teaching more than a thousand seminar attendees and condenses it for you. In a handy problem/solution format, he includes tips for installing IIS and Visual InterDev; pointers for using ASP, database applications, and COM components; tips for optimizing IIS performance; tips for troubleshooting IIS and Visual InterDev security; and more. 168 pages.

Also Published by 29th Street Press

1001 SECRETS FOR WINDOWS NT REGISTRY

By Tim Daniels

For the accomplished user, *1001 Secrets for Windows NT Registry* is the definitive reference for system customization and optimization. Organized into sections that cover networking, applications, system management, hardware, and performance, the book also has an accompanying CD that is packed with innovative registry monitoring and performance utilities. 321 pages.

THE ADMINISTRATOR'S GUIDE TO MICROSOFT SQL SERVER 6.5

By Kevin Cox and William Jones

This book guides database managers and administrators into a thorough understanding of the client/server aspects of the SQL Server 6.5 product, and includes many useful tips for managing security, troubleshooting, and improving performance. 469 pages.

BUILDING AS/400 CLIENT/SERVER APPLICATIONS
Put ODBC and Client Access APIs to Work

By Mike Otey

Mike Otey gives you the why, what, and how-to of AS/400 client/server computing, which matches the strengths of the AS/400 with the PC GUIs that users want. This book's clear and easy-to-understand style guides you through all the important aspects of AS/400 client/server applications. Mike covers APPC and TCP/IP communications, as well as the underlying architectures for each of the major AS/400 client/server APIs. CD with complete source code for several working applications included. 505 pages.

CONTROL LANGUAGE PROGRAMMING FOR THE AS/400, SECOND EDITION

By Bryan Meyers and Dan Riehl, NEWS/400 technical editors

This comprehensive CL programming textbook offers students up-to-the-minute knowledge of the skills they will need in today's MIS environment. Chapters progress methodically from CL basics to more complex processes and concepts, guiding students toward a professional grasp of CL programming techniques and style. In this second edition, the authors have updated the text to include discussion of the Integrated Language Environment (ILE) and the fundamental changes ILE introduces to the AS/400's execution model. 522 pages.

DATABASE DESIGN AND PROGRAMMING FOR DB2/400

By Paul Conte

This textbook is the most complete guide to DB2/400 design and programming available anywhere. The author shows you everything you need to know about physical and logical file DDS, SQL/400, and RPG IV and COBOL/400 database programming. Each programming chapter includes a specific list of "Coding Suggestions" that will help you write faster and more maintainable code. In addition, the author provides an extensive section on practical database design for DB2/400. 610 pages.

DDS PROGRAMMING FOR DISPLAY & PRINTER FILES

By James Coolbaugh

Offers a thorough, straightforward explanation of how to use Data Description Specifications (DDS) to program display files and printer files. Covers basic to complex tasks using DDS functions. The author uses DDS programming examples for CL and RPG extensively throughout the book, and you can put these examples to use immediately. A complimentary diskette includes all the source code presented in the book. 444 pages.

DATA WAREHOUSING AND THE AS/400

By Scott Steinacher

In this book, Scott Steinacher takes an in-depth look at data-warehousing components, concepts, and terminology. After laying this foundation, Scott presents a compelling case for implementing a data warehouse on the AS/400. Included on an accompanying CD are demos of AS/400 data-warehousing software from several independent software vendors. 342 pages.

DEVELOPING YOUR AS/400 INTERNET STRATEGY

By Alan Arnold

This book addresses the issues unique to deploying your AS/400 on the Internet. It includes procedures for configuring AS/400 TCP/IP and information about which client and server technologies the AS/400 supports natively. This enterprise-class tutorial evaluates the AS/400 as an Internet server and teaches you how to design, program, and manage your Web home page. 248 pages.

ESSENTIALS OF SUBFILE PROGRAMMING
and Advanced Topics in RPG

By Phil Levinson

Essentials of Subfile Programming teaches you to design and program subfiles, offering step-by-step instructions and real-world programming exercises that build from chapter to chapter. You learn to design and create subfile records; load, clear, and display subfiles; and create pop-up windows. In addition, the advanced topics help you mine the rich store of data in the file-information and program-status data structures, handle errors, improve data integrity, and manage program-to-program communication. An instructor's manual is available. 260 pages.

IMPLEMENTING AS/400 SECURITY, THIRD EDITION

By Wayne Madden and Carol Woodbury

Concise and practical, this third edition of *Implementing AS/400 Security* not only brings together in one place the fundamental AS/400 security tools and experience-based recommendations that you need, but also includes specifics on the latest security enhancements available in OS/400 V4R1 and V4R2. In addition, you will find completely new chapters that include discussions about Internet security and business contingency planning. 424 pages.

INSIDE THE AS/400, SECOND EDITION
Featuring the AS/400e series

By Frank G. Soltis

Learn from the architect of the AS/400 about the new generation of AS/400e systems and servers, and about the latest system features and capabilities introduced in Version 4 of OS/400. Dr. Frank Soltis demystifies the system, shedding light on how it came to be, how it can do the things it does, and what its future may hold. 402 pages.

INTERNET SECURITY WITH WINDOWS NT

By Mark Joseph Edwards

Security expert and *Windows NT Magazine* news editor Mark Edwards provides the quintessential guide to Internet and intranet security from the Windows NT platform. This comprehensive book covers network security basics as well as IIS and MPS, and includes specific advice about selecting NT tools and security devices. The accompanying CD-ROM includes security-related utilities, tools, and software packages that, combined with the tips and techniques in the book, are powerful weapons in your security efforts. 520 pages.

AN INTRODUCTION TO AS/400 SYSTEM OPERATIONS

By Patrice Gapen and Heidi Rothenbuehler

Here's the textbook that covers what you need to know to become a successful AS/400 system operator. *Introduction to AS/400 System Operations* covers a broad range of topics, including system architecture; DB2/400 and Query; user interface and Operational Assistant; managing jobs and printed reports; backup and restore; system configuration and networks; performance; security; and Client Access (PC Support). 233 pages.

MASTERING AS/400 PERFORMANCE

By Alan Arnold, Charly Jones, Jim Stewart, and Rick Turner

In *Mastering AS/400 Performance*, the experts tell you how to measure, evaluate, and tune your AS/400's performance. From the authors' experience in the field, they give you techniques for improving performance beyond simply buying additional hardware. Learn the techniques, gain the insight, and help your company profit from the experience of the top AS/400 performance professionals in the country. 259 pages.

THE MICROSOFT EXCHANGE SERVER INTERNET MAIL CONNECTOR

By Spyros Sakellariadis

Achieve Internet connectivity using Exchange Server 4.0 and 5.0. This book presents four Internet connectivity models, shows how to set up the Internet Mail Connector with an Internet Service Provider, and illustrates how to monitor Internet traffic. It also includes troubleshooting and reference guides. 234 pages.

THE MICROSOFT EXCHANGE USER'S HANDBOOK

By Sue Mosher

Microsoft Exchange is all about making connections — connections to a Microsoft Mail server, to Exchange Server, to a fax machine, or to online services. Here's the must-have, complete guide for users who need to know how to set up and use all the features of the Microsoft Exchange client product. Includes chapters about Microsoft Exchange Server 5.0 and Microsoft Outlook. 692 pages. CD included.

THE MICROSOFT OUTLOOK E-MAIL AND FAX GUIDE

By Sue Mosher

Sue Mosher explains the setup of individual e-mail services and components, e-mail options and when you might want to use them, and many time-saving techniques that take you beyond the basics. Users at all levels will learn from this comprehensive introduction to Microsoft's next generation of messaging software. The book includes coverage of the Internet Mail Enhancement Patch, Rules Wizard, and special features for Microsoft Exchange Server users. 500 pages.

MIGRATING TO WINDOWS NT 4.0

By Sean Daily

This book is a comprehensive yet concise guide to the significant changes users will encounter as they make the move to Windows NT 4.0. The author, a Microsoft Certified Systems Engineer (MCSE), eases the transition with a wealth of tips and techniques that give readers the sense they're receiving "insider information." 475 pages.

POWERING YOUR WEB SITE WITH WINDOWS NT SERVER

By Nik Simpson

Powering Your Web Site with Windows NT Server explores the tools necessary to establish a presence on the Internet or on an internal corporate intranet using Web technology and Windows NT Server. The author helps readers navigate the process of creating a new information infrastructure, from the basics of justifying the decision to management through the complete implementation cycle. 640 pages. CD included.

PROGRAMMING IN RPG IV, REVISED EDITION

By Judy Yaeger, Ph.D., a NEWS/400 technical editor

This textbook provides a strong foundation in the essentials of business programming, featuring the newest version of the RPG language: RPG IV. Focusing on real-world problems and down-to-earth solutions using the latest techniques and features of RPG, this book provides everything you need to know to write a well-designed RPG IV program. This revised edition includes a new section about subprocedures and an addition about using the RPG ILE source debugger. An instructor's kit is available. 435 pages.

PROGRAMMING IN RPG/400, SECOND EDITION

By Judy Yaeger, Ph.D., a NEWS/400 technical editor

This second edition refines and extends the comprehensive instructional material contained in the original textbook and features a new section that introduces externally described printer files, a new chapter that highlights the fundamentals of RPG IV, and a new appendix that correlates the key concepts from each chapter with their RPG IV counterparts. The book includes everything you need to learn how to write a well-designed RPG program. An instructor's kit is available. 481 pages.

RPG IV BY EXAMPLE

By George Farr and Shailan Topiwala

RPG IV by Example addresses the needs and concerns of RPG programmers at any level of experience. The focus is on RPG IV in a practical context that lets AS/400 professionals quickly grasp what's new without dwelling on the old. Beginning with an overview of RPG IV specifications, the authors prepare the way for examining all the features of the new version of the language. The chapters that follow explore RPG IV further with practical, easy-to-use applications. 488 pages.

RPG/400 INTERACTIVE TEMPLATE TECHNIQUE
By Carson Soule, CDP, CCP, CSP

The book shows you time-saving, program-sharpening concepts behind the template approach, and includes all the code you need to build one perfect program after another. These templates include code for cursor-sensitive prompting in DDS, for handling messages in resident RPG programs, for using the CLEAR opcode to eliminate hard-coded field initialization, and much more. There's even a new select template with a pop-up window. 234 pages.

USING QUERY/400
By Patrice Gapen and Catherine Stoughton

This textbook, designed for any AS/400 user from student to professional with or without prior programming knowledge, presents Query as an easy and fast tool for creating reports and files from AS/400 databases. Topics include defining database files to Query, selecting and sequencing fields, generating new numeric and character fields, joining database files, defining custom headings, creating new database files, and more. Instructor's kit available. 92 pages.

VISUALAGE FOR RPG BY EXAMPLE
By Bryan Meyers and Jef Sutherland

VisualAge for RPG by Example brings the RPG language to the GUI world and lets you use your existing knowledge to develop Windows applications. Using a tutorial approach, *VisualAge for RPG by Example* lets you learn as you go and create simple yet functional programs start to finish. The accompanying CD-ROM offers a scaled down version of VARPG and complete source code for the sample project. 236 pages.

WINDOWS NT MAGAZINE ADMINISTRATOR'S SURVIVAL GUIDE: SYSTEM MANAGEMENT AND SECURITY
Edited by John Enck

In this first book in our Survival Guide™ series, John Enck has assembled the best articles and authors from *Windows NT Magazine* to share their experience with mission-critical system management and security issues. Topics include optimization, tuning, troubleshooting, programming, installation, securing the Internet connection, testing, firewalls, data access, task managers, file servers, passwords, authentication, and more. 359 pages.

WINDOWS NT MAGAZINE ADMINISTRATOR'S SURVIVAL GUIDE: NETWORKING AND BACKOFFICE
Edited by John Enck

In this second book in our Survival Guide™ series, John Enck has assembled the best *Windows NT Magazine* articles about networking and BackOffice issues. Topics include assigning IP addresses and IP routing; name resolution with WINS, NetBIOS, and DNS; using NT with the Internet; NT Services for Macintosh; connectivity; clusters; enhancing SQL Server performance; implementing MS Exchange; Systems Management Server; and more. 469 pages.

FOR A COMPLETE CATALOG OR TO PLACE AN ORDER, CONTACT

29th Street Press
Duke Communications International
221 E. 29th Street • Loveland, CO 80538-2727
(800) 621-1544 • (970) 663-4700 • Fax: (970) 203-2756

OR SHOP OUR WEB SITE: **www.29thStreetPress.com**

We Want Your Response

Mail it

Fax it

Web it

Complete this form to join our network of computer professionals

We'll gladly send you a free copy of

- ❏ *Windows NT Magazine*
- ❏ *NEWS/400*
- ❏ *Selling AS/400 Solutions*
- ❏ *Business Finance*

Name _____

Title _____ Phone _____

Company _____

Address _____

City/State/Zip _____

E-mail _____

Where did you purchase this book?

❏ Trade show ❏ Computer store ❏ Internet ❏ Card deck ❏ Bookstore

❏ Magazine ❏ Direct mail catalog or brochure

What new applications do you expect to use during the next year?

_____

_____

How many times this month will you visit one of Duke Communication's Web sites (29th Street Press, NEWS/400, Selling AS/400 Solutions, Windows NT Magazine, Business Finance)**?** _____

Please share your reaction to The AS/400 Expert: Ready-to-Run RPG/400 Techniques _____

_____

_____

❏ YES! You have my permission to quote my comments in your publications.
(initials) _____

[98SCXBOOK]

COPY THIS PAGE AND MAIL TO

29TH STREET PRESS • 221 EAST 29TH STREET • LOVELAND, CO 80538

OR FAX TO (970) 667-2321

OR RESPOND VIA OUR WEB SITE AT www.29thStreetPress.com

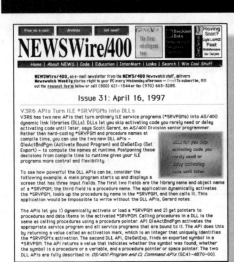